LIFE AND DEATH AT ABBEY GATE

The Fall of Afghanistan and the Operation to Save our Allies

MIKAEL COOK
with ROBERT CONLIN

CASEMATE
Philadelphia & Oxford

Published in the United States of America and Great Britain in 2023 by
CASEMATE PUBLISHERS
1950 Lawrence Road, Havertown, PA 19083, USA
and
The Old Music Hall, 106–108 Cowley Road, Oxford OX4 1JE, UK

Copyright 2023 © Mikael Cook with Robert Conlin

Paperback Edition: ISBN 978-1-63624-396-2
Digital Edition: ISBN 978-1-63624-397-9

A CIP record for this book is available from the British Library

All rights reserved. No part of this book may be reproduced or transmitted in any form or by any means, electronic or mechanical including photocopying, recording or by any information storage and retrieval system, without permission from the publisher in writing.

Printed and bound in the United Kingdom by CPI Group (UK) Ltd, Croydon, CR0 4YY

Typeset in India by Lapiz Digital Services, Chennai.

For a complete list of Casemate titles, please contact:

CASEMATE PUBLISHERS (US)
Telephone (610) 853-9131
Fax (610) 853-9146
Email: casemate@casematepublishers.com
www.casematepublishers.com

CASEMATE PUBLISHERS (UK)
Telephone (0)1226 734350
Email: casemate-uk@casematepublishers.co.uk
www.casematepublishers.co.uk

Disclaimer
This book is based on actual events. However, some names have been changed to protect U.S. service members still active, as well as some Afghans still in harm's way.

My friends, Abdul and Mohammad, both have family back in Kabul and have asked me to use their first names only to protect them from retaliation by the Taliban.

The views expressed in this publication are those of the author and do not necessarily reflect the official policy or position of the Department of Defense or the U.S. government. The public release clearance of this publication by the Department of Defense does not imply Department of Defense endorsement or factual accuracy of the material.

Original cover by Rafael Kotyrba.

This book is dedicated to our Afghan allies who stood next to us for 20 long years of war, who were promised protection, then left behind.
To the 13 American heroes who made the ultimate sacrifice at Abbey Gate, Hamid Karzai International Airport. Your courage and humanity will never be forgotten.
Thank you for helping save my friends.

Contents

Foreword   vii
Prologue: Abbey Gate, HKIA   xi
Preface: What Was #DigitalDunkirk?   xvii

1	At Home in Michigan	1
2	An Ann Arbor Childhood	5
3	Basic Training	11
4	Deployment	15
5	A Kabul Childhood	25
6	Early Summer 2021	31
7	Marines Make their Way to HKIA	39
8	Underway With *#DigitalDunkirk*	49
9	Abbey Gate	57
10	Team Wins—Getting Them Out	71
11	The Blast	89
12	The Mission Continues—The Paiman Rescue	101
13	The Aftermath	123

Foreword

When Tom Schueman called me in April 2021, I detected a sense of desperation in his voice that unsettled me. A proven combat leader with steady resolve, Tom led patrols in Afghanistan's deadly Helmand Valley in 2011 while he served in 3rd Battalion, 5th Marine Regiment—the famed "Darkhorse" Battalion. There he confronted unspeakable horrors among the deadliest fighting in the U.S. Marine Corps' storied history. In all the time I had known him, Tom was not one to let his emotions shake his constitution. This was different. Tom needed my help.

Over the next few moments, Tom explained to me the meticulous efforts he had already made—over the course of years—to secure a Special Immigration Visa for his former Afghan interpreter, Zak. Through the cauldron of combat, Tom had forged a bond with Zak that was indistinguishable from a family tie. They were brothers. He would sacrifice anything for Zak, and Zak would do the same for him. After he painstakingly exhausted all official channels through the U.S. State Department, Tom explained that the Taliban were now hunting Zak and his family as they perilously trekked through back-channels in Afghanistan on their way to Kabul. Tom thought that my training as a lawyer and my dedication to duty as a fellow Marine would prove a potent combination to create a miracle out of an impossibly desperate situation. The unspoken truth between us was that if we failed, Zak and his family would die.

Nearly every day for the next four months we worked in a methodical manner. We wrote letters to elected officials, completed government documents, filed appeals, spoke to reporters, consulted immigrations experts, and filled social media with posts that could be shared with a growing number of concerned service members and young veterans. We experienced some success, receiving endorsements for our efforts—and for Zak's service to the United States—from key leaders in the administration, but what neither of us could anticipate was that we would soon repeat this process over and over in unimaginable and quickening succession without achieving our goal: bringing Zak and his family to safety. As we talked, the world watched with white knuckles as the Taliban corralled thousands of desperate Afghans in and around the Hamid Karzai International Airport (HKIA) during those harrowing days in August 2021. Our process, however imperfectly created during that fateful summer, would soon ripple across a community of patriots who believed in an unspoken obligation and duty to our Afghan partners.

Rarely in one's life will a person truly understand what they are capable of accomplishing. In his classic book *Profiles in Courage*, John F. Kennedy remarked: "Great crises produce great men." It is under the highest pressures that one's training and character are revealed—or at least stripped of the veneer of modern life. In this book you will not only learn of the extraordinary efforts of *#DigitalDunkirk*—an effort no less epic in its scale and impact than that of the remarkable Brits that etched its namesake into history books in 1940—but you will learn of the impact of the finest men and women that this nation has to offer. The Marines, soldiers, and sailors who bravely defended our country's greatest ideals and snatched desperate Afghans from the jaws of Taliban terrorists are precisely the people whose stories must be told by our generation. In an era so desperately in need of heroes, this book provides the reader with many.

But why were so many moved to act? How could they sense their efforts would matter? After all, *#DigitalDunkirk* mobilized a community that transcended the ranks of our veteran community. The British civilian fishing boats of 1940 were replaced with an instrument of immeasurable power, capable of orchestrating full-scale evacuation operations from half a world away: the smartphone. Anyone with an iPhone was capable of rowing towards the digital shore in Kabul to help. And they did. So, maybe, it was merely access that made it easier to provide help? However, in my estimation, the call to act and the outpouring of genuine support originated in a much more fundamentally important way.

Pondering over this for the last year, I came to realize there's an even more captivating moral that comes to life within the pages of *Life and Death at Abbey Gate*. That is that sometimes our most impressive achievements are the result of collaborative effort, of which we have little knowledge at the time and might never fully comprehend our impact. Arguably, no organization in history has successfully harnessed the spirit of unity of purpose more than the professional military. From the co-dependency of the Roman phalanx to the modern "Code of Conduct," as service members we fundamentally believe we are each other's keepers – in every sense of the word.

Determined to tell the story of *#DigitalDunkirk* and the exceptional heroism at Abbey Gate, Mikael Cook pored over numerous accounts of those efforts, interviewed dozens of individuals with first-hand knowledge, and pulled together a crucial timeline of events in order to fully demonstrate the impact. In these pages, Mikael highlights the story most of us who were part of the effort knew had to be told. Maybe it is a failure to grasp the interwoven web and rippled effects of our actions, or maybe our group (which consists mostly of service members) have been bred to simply accept that we were doing our duty for which no special plaudits are required. In the end, the task of telling *our* story and placing it upon the mantel, to be appropriately judged, has begun. Did we measure up to the crises?

A former great citizen-soldier once offered that the United States has two fundamental powers: the power of intimidation toward our enemies and the power of inspiration towards our friends. No better friend, no worse enemy. Each of us believed then, as we believe now, that we were acting consistently with those policies or expectations of our Oath and the administration's promise "to keep faith" with our partners and allies. Through all modern conflict's complexity, our imperative is not simply to win. It is to win with honor, that is, to maintain legitimacy—the moral high ground in victory. Military forces must be legitimate if they are to be effective. Reputation matters. Adding to the challenge, professional military forces must be legitimate both in the conduct of their operations and in the perception of that conduct by numerous, disparate, interconnected audiences around the world. No matter how our enemies attempt to weaponize our adherence to our principles—even when we fall short—we act in a manner that acknowledges, for all time, ours is the greatest nation the world has ever known.

Life and Death at Abbey Gate is published at a time when our nation sits at a crossroads. Partisan rancor rules the day and stifles meaningful progress. Similarly, the U.S. military, not actively engaged in combat operations for the first time in two decades, now epitomizes the criticisms of a "garrison" force, under-employed and in-fighting over its identity and future design. Yet, here emerges a story that confirms: It is worth it. "It" being the ethos and principles upon which the United States has forged its reputation.

Life and Death at Abbey Gate demonstrates, in a deeply personal account, how each of us can make a difference. This book serves as a stark example to the entire world that there is nothing that Americans are incapable of doing when we work together. In those values we share and cultivate as Americans we can, in measurable ways, have deep and lasting impacts on the entire world. It symbolizes that there is literally nothing that can stop an American committed to a just cause. As you read the pages of this book—and many like it that should be written—you will be struck by two interrelated realizations. First, that that you are capable of more than you know, so go for it. Second, that our nation's best days are still ahead of us, so long as we remain true to our founding principles and work together. If you doubt either, *Life and Death at Abbey Gate* will convince you.

Christopher Davis
Washington, D.C.
July 2023

PROLOGUE

Abbey Gate, HKIA

"Break Break Break."

The encrypted Signal chat room I was logged into the morning of August 25, 2021 barked out the universal military command to stand down and pay attention because something important was about to come through. Again.

I slumped in my chair at my computer desk in southeast Michigan and watched in an exhausted stupor as the ongoing drama that's come to be known as *#DigitalDunkirk* played out on the screen.

"Reports of S-vest [suicide vest] en route to Abbey Gate."

When I first saw a message like this, days before, I felt my blood run cold. But by this point, I had barely slept in four days, and this was yet another report of a possible suicide vest attack at the most crowded gate at the Hamid Karzai International Airport (HKIA) in Kabul, Afghanistan.

Safe in my own house 7,000 miles away, I could choose to ignore the danger. I could close my eyes and drift off while the chat room lit up. But I didn't. I had made a life-or-death promise to my Afghan friends, Abdul and Mohammad, to help get them out of the country, and sleep was not an option.

So I fought back the waves of fatigue and refocused. This chaotic ongoing evacuation of American citizens and our Afghan allies was extremely personal to every Afghanistan campaign veteran in America, and I was no exception. The fact that my Afghan friends were in the midst of this crisis intensified that feeling even more.

The Marines of the 2nd Battalion, 1st Marine Regiment (2/1) who manned the gate didn't have the luxury of giving in to their exhaustion, or ignoring the overwhelming stench of human waste and death, or the cries of despair from mothers holding their terrified children. While they engaged in the largest and most chaotic civilian evacuation in U.S. history, they also had to contend with the threat of an attack by an enemy both seen and unseen.

In the days leading up to August 26, 2021, the command post at HKIA issued 60 credible reports of potential ISIS-K suicide bombers roaming the perimeter of the airport intent on having one last crack at killing Americans before they left Afghanistan forever. They would be happy to take any Afghans fleeing in terror with them as well. To them, these Afghans weren't countrymen; they were infidels.

The threat reports were increasing with frequency as the clock ticked towards the August 31 midnight deadline for the Taliban's official takeover of the country and everything and everyone in it. By the 25th, the sixth sense in the #DigitalDunkirk chat seemed to morph from dread to resigned fatalism. It seemed like it was just a matter of time; the fifth trigger pull of a six-shot revolver in a game of Russian roulette.

As they worked to keep the increasingly desperate crowds from storming the airfield again and putting a halt to the massive evacuation effort, Sergeant Ethan Zielinski and his squad from 2/1 Weapons Company were laser-focused on trying to prevent an IED incident. But their attention was being pulled in every direction at the same time.

For one, their mission of strictly providing security at the gate had evolved into a multi-pronged effort that included non-lethal crowd control, threat recognition, and the attention-consuming and dangerous job of screening which Afghans were eligible for the golden ticket to America that they were risking their lives and the lives of their family to get. This necessary proximity didn't allow the Marines to establish a buffer zone to help mitigate any threats.

The sound of gunshots rang out in staccato bursts constantly as Taliban gunmen, who manned an outer checkpoint that led to the main gate, fired into the air to harass and intimidate the terrified crowd. The Marines, some of whom had combat experience battling the Taliban on previous deployments, found themselves in the surreal position of standing nearly shoulder to shoulder with their former foes to accomplish the mission.

Abdul Hadi Hamdan, a Taliban commander leading troops at HKIA, claimed to have over 1,000 fighters wearing suicide vests patrolling the airport. Sergeant Zielinski watched one of them intently as the military-aged male fidgeted with a cell phone connected to what appeared to be wires leading into his chest rig. The rules of engagement prevented him from reacting unless there was an imminent threat to Marines. He watched as the man melted away in the crowd. Sergeant Tyler Vargas-Andrews, a sniper from 2/1 Weapons Company, had a military-aged male who fit the description of the bomber sighted in his scope. He requested permission to engage from his battalion commander after the psychological operations team confirmed the target, but the request was denied.

All of this would have been daunting even if they had been trained for it. These were United States Marines. One of the most—if not *the* most—highly trained and lethal fighting forces in the world. Of course they had trained for the mission. They trained for everything.

Not Sergeant Zielinski's Weapons Company. In the plane on the way over from Ali Al Salem Airbase in Kuwait City he heard some other companies talking about the non-lethal crowd control training they received, but his five-member team, an 81mm mortar squad, had gotten last-minute orders to come from Kuwait, where they had been deployed since April.

Their training for this once-in-a-generation mission—a chaotic mass evacuation of American non-combatants and their allies in a hostile environment, which hadn't been seen since the fall of Saigon in 1975—had been fairly minimal due to the expedited timing. To make up for the short workup time, they conducted drills on the tarmac while waiting for the plane.

As they monitored radio traffic about suicide bomb threats and pushed back the crowd, they also juggled cell phone calls and texts from American veterans, politicians and people connected to them, NGO (non-governmental organization) officials and a hodgepodge of frantic, faceless people.

The messages were a variation of the same theme: "My interpreter [or other support personnel] is at the gate with his family. The Taliban will kill them if they're discovered. Please help me get them out."

The Marine would climb up onto the canal wall, a Jersey barrier, or any elevated position within the Abbey Gate sector and look out into the mass of humanity to try and spot these people. Thousands of people filled every inch of available space. Some waved identifying handwritten placards, or a colorful scarf; anything to help distinguish them. Others didn't. It could be like looking for the proverbial needle in a haystack.

If that wasn't difficult enough, it didn't help that an EOD (Explosive Ordnance Disposal) team was blanketing the Abbey Gate sector with electronic jamming signals, which would block a remote-controlled detonation but were useless against self-detonating suicide vest bombs. The devices interrupted cell phone connections, causing many of the long-distance calls to drop and whatever progress might have been made between the caller on one end and the Marine on the other to drop with them.

The Taliban were also using jamming devices in an attempt to cause more disruption. On paper, they were supposed to be providing security to allow the evacuation to flow unimpeded until the deadline, but Sergeant Zielinski and others noted the sadistic glee some of them displayed in their new role as conquerors. They would see evidence of this too many times to count.

If the hand of fortune kept the phone line open and provided a Marine a confirmed visual of the targets, they still needed to wade into the crowd to get to them, check to see if they had the correct paperwork (which constantly changed depending on the latest orders from the State Department) and then get them back through the resentful crowd at the gate to the processing center at the PAX terminal.

I didn't know any of these details when my friend, Abdul, handed his phone to Sergeant Ethan Zielinski from Elmhurst, Illinois. All I knew was that Abdul, Mohammad, their wives and five young children under the age of eight had made it to Abbey Gate after a harrowing journey from a Kabul neighborhood.

But that was only half the battle. Now that they were there, I still had to get them past the gate, in the airport, and on a plane.

When Abdul handed the phone to Zielinski, they were wedged into a shit-filled sewage canal in between a wall of humanity. The Marines stood on a wall above them. It was almost exactly the spot where the very next day an ISIS bomber would pull the trigger and detonate a bomb that killed 13 American troops and over 170 Afghan civilians.

The day before, Abdul didn't know Sergeant Zielinski and Zielinski didn't know him. When I identified myself to him over the balky phone line, I didn't know Sergeant Zielinksi and he didn't know me.

Yet here we are, close to two years later, telling the story together. This is our story. It's also the story of U.S. Army Specialist Bismillah Paiman and his family, who bravely dodged the Taliban for a month before finding their way to America.

It's the story too of Sergeant Jose Ramirez, Sergeant Kasey Williamson, Lance Corporal Caden Bair and Corporal Corey Moore, all 2/1 Marines who faithfully manned their posts at the hell that's known as Abbey Gate and are willing to relive the experience to convey the story through their eyes.

It's a story about the courage, fortitude and sacrifice of the U.S. service members who died, and the ones who survived and still carry the physical and emotional scars of that mission.

It's not the story of a shameful American betrayal of our Afghan allies, or unbelievably inept bureaucracy, or political finger-pointing. Plenty of others have and will tell that story, and will bend the narrative to fit their agenda. All of it happened, but that's not the story I'm telling.

This story is also about the Afghan allies who endured incredible hardship in the hopes of building a life in the United States. As a result of my involvement, there are 20 of them living free of fear in our country now. Of the millions of Afghans who had this dream, they are the lucky ones. As depressing as the details of the story can be sometimes, that's the silver lining I can never forget.

Last, but not least, this is a story about the spontaneous act of human decency, unflagging determination and American ingenuity that came to be known as *#DigitalDunkirk*. For the hundreds of people who poured their blood, sweat and tears into helping evacuate 124,000 people in 15 days, this is your story too.

PREFACE

What Was *#DigitalDunkirk?*

Even today, nearly two years after it happened, I'm still almost at a loss for words when I try to describe what it was like to take part in *#DigitalDunkirk*. But it's not an option to be at a loss for words when you're writing a book about the subject, so I'll do my best to explain it.

Let's start with my biggest takeaway: *#DigitalDunkirk* restored my faith in humanity. With all the divisiveness in the United States today—much of which is promoted, exploited and spread on the same digital platforms that made *#DigitalDunkirk* possible—it's still incredible to me that so many people with such different backgrounds and beliefs could rally together to achieve the impossible.

The group's name, *#DigitalDunkirk*, was inspired by the historic World War II evacuation effort, when hundreds of British civilian boats assisted the British Royal Navy in evacuating Allied troops in danger of annihilation by the German Army from the French beaches of Dunkirk. In total, 338,226 troops were rescued and brought back to England.

This time around, we didn't have boats, nor beaches, and we weren't saving our own troops. We had cell phones, computers, and social media, and we were saving our Afghan friends.

The fact that it happened completely organically, with no command structure or hierarchy, and there was hardly any evidence of ego or self-promotion, made it seem like some kind of fairy tale about a lost civilization where people put their own needs aside and went above and beyond to help others in need because it was just and worthy.

Many of us found ourselves entering this group in the same fashion—by accident. Most of us tried the proper government channels, filling out the required paperwork, only to be told, "Just have them shelter in place for now." But this mission was personal for most of us, and we knew that wasn't the solution. These were our friends' lives, and they were being hunted by a brutal enemy. So we set up shop on the internet. We started assembling teams of anyone and everyone who could help. From alphabet soup entities such as CIA and NSA agents, to military veterans who served in Afghanistan, to congressional staffers and many more.

Individually, we brought little more than the name of the Afghans we wanted to help and our varied experience and skills, but collectively we formed a formidable army. It was all these people dropping everything in their life for a week, two weeks, three weeks and more, to get this done. With almost no sleep the whole time, because falling asleep might mean an urgent missed message between them and a facilitator on the other end in Kabul. Catnaps with one eye open became the default sleeping method.

We started setting up TOCs (Tactical Operations Centers) and creating message threads on encrypted messaging apps such as Signal to pass information. Group members might have been texting and talking with someone on the ground at HKIA, drawing on the constantly updated intel and resources out in the dozens of dedicated chat rooms to provide updated information on gates that may have just closed, or routes to avoid Taliban patrols, or visual signals to use to get the attention of a Marine at the gates.

Or they could have been talking with a Marine at HKIA, trying desperately to reach across the thousands of miles that separated them to give them some nugget of information that could help them identify and then escort the person or persons they were trying to help.

They may have been reaching across their own network of personal and professional connections to find someone with information on available charter flights, on what it took to get on a flight manifest, on Special Immigrant Visa (SIV) document requirements, on family eligibility, or on what other countries might be accepting applicants.

Or they could have been involved in raising money for those charter flights, or finding pilots to fly them and crews to help the hundreds of exhausted people when they finally boarded them.

Maybe they were talking with congressional aides in D.C. or contacts at the State Department or DHS to try and get help. Or they heard about an NGO that had a valuable high-level contact and chased that tiger's tail until they found them or exhausted themselves trying. If anyone had a breakthrough, or discovered a workaround, they'd put it out on the chat rooms and then answer the hundreds of messages they'd be bombarded with right after it hit the airwaves.

Let's not forget this all happened in the dog days of summer, when most people are at the beach or the lake, the camp, BBQs, family gatherings, getting a break from the daily grind. The last thing anyone is looking to do in August is stay indoors glued to their phone day and night.

Many, like me, got involved because they knew a specific Afghan who was eligible to get out. Many did not. They put their life on hold in the sweltering heat of August because it was the right thing to do. They recognized that our American values were at stake and our government had inexplicably dropped the ball, so they would need to pick it up and run with it.

Throughout August and beyond, *#DigitalDunkirk* is credited with helping evacuate 124,000 Americans and Afghan allies. This is a record for a civilian airlift evacuation that probably won't be broken any time soon.

The fact a Hollywood remake of a movie about the original Dunkirk evacuation was a box-office hit nearly 80 years after it happened is testimony to how unique that mission was. It remains in the public consciousness because there haven't been too many examples in human history when the public gets to rescue the military. That wasn't the exact case in Kabul, but there were enough similarities to understand how the name *#DigitalDunkirk* came about.

Though the strategy and execution was much different than the original Dunkirk rescue in 1940, one thing remained the same: the human desire to help one another in a time of need. I think it's a much-needed reminder of what we can accomplish when we put our differences aside, and just see each other as people unified by the principles of freedom, democracy and honor.

Hopefully, people will still remember it happened 80 years from now.

CHAPTER I

At Home in Michigan

It's a Sunday night in early October in Ypsilanti, Michigan. There's a chill in the air now, and leaves have been dropping from the trees and swirling in the autumn gusts that come down from Canada like clockwork every year to signal the change of seasons.

I've just come back from my friend Abdul's house. Which means that I'm well fed and played out, because another thing I can count on is that almost every Sunday evening I'm in town, I will have eaten a platter of delicious Afghan food and played with the cutest kids this side of Kabul.

I don't really have a choice in the matter. Refusing the hospitality of an Afghan is a high crime and misdemeanor, even if you're over there as often as I am. When you step foot in an Afghan house, you're treated like the most important person on the planet. I've learned to stop reflexively refusing and just accept it.

When I explain our friendship, you might think I get preferential treatment because of it, but I guarantee that's not the case. I could have been some guy on a work release program from prison and they'd treat me the same way.

When I arrived that evening, Abdul spoke the customary Afghan greeting by asking, "Brother, how's your family?" Afghans are obsessed with being polite and gracious hosts.

"How is my family? My family is great, Abdul." I ask him the same, and he says they're fine, but I know that's not entirely true. I know that the culture shock of being here has been hard on all of them. He, his wife and kids all have a new language to learn. He had to get a driver's license, and they all have had to learn new customs that are second nature to us. He has to work long hours to afford an apartment and pay for necessities.

He's worried about his family back in Kabul and the misery the Taliban is inflicting on all of them he left behind. He wires money back from every paycheck because the economy has cratered in Kabul, and without it they won't have enough to eat. I know he especially misses his younger brother, Massoud, who hoped to come with him, but who got separated in the chaos at the airport. He prays that he'll see him again someday.

But Abdul is alive. His children are growing. If all goes right with the immigration process still ahead, they'll make their way here and hopefully live the American dream like so many immigrants before them. We almost turned our backs on them. We almost shut the door in their faces. But, thank God, we didn't.

Now we can tell the story of his journey and the journey of all the Afghans who managed to get out of Kabul. We can let people know that although the bright lights of the media have shifted to other conflicts and events, the effort still continues.

We can give the 2/1 Marines who were there at Abbey Gate the chance to tell us in their words what that was like. They're the ones who carry the physical and emotional scars of the experience. The rest of us are just bystanders.

Finally and most regrettably, we can do our best to honor the ultimate sacrifice of the 13 U.S. service members who died at Abbey Gate at HKIA the day after Abdul and Mohammad left. They are:

> Staff Sergeant Darin Hoover, 2/1 Marines
> Sergeant Johnny Rosario-Pichardo, 5th Marine Expeditionary Brigade
> Sergeant Nicole Gee, 24th Marine Expeditionary Unit
> Corporal Hunter Lopez, 2/1 Marines
> Corporal Daegan Page, 2/1 Marines
> Corporal Humberto Sanchez, 2/1 Marines
> Lance Corporal David Espinoza, 2/1 Marines
> Lance Corporal Jared Schmitz, 2/1 Marines

Lance Corporal Rylee McCollum, 2/1 Marines
Lance Corporal Dylan Merola, 2/1 Marines
Lance Corporal Kareem Nikoui, 2/1 Marines
Navy Corpsman Maxton Soviak, attached to 2/1 Marines
Army Staff Sergeant Ryan Knauss, 8th PSYOP Group

The hand of fate brought us all together in August 2021, and lives were forever changed or ended by small units of measure; a few seconds before or after, a few feet this way or that. Life or death. Freedom or enslavement. As I watched Abdul's and Mohammad's beautiful kids playing tonight, I thought about how lucky we are to be able to tell this story.

CHAPTER 2

An Ann Arbor Childhood

Every book has a beginning, and every life does too, so I may as well start at the beginning of mine and give you an idea of who I am and how I ended up in the position of telling this story.

I was born in 1989 in Ann Arbor, Michigan, the second of two sons. My dad, Robin, ran a moving company with his brother when I was born. Dad came from a well-to-do, but pretty dysfunctional family from Beaver, PA, located 30 miles northwest of Pittsburgh. Back in the day, the Cooks made their money breeding and raising Belgian horses for the Belgian royal family, as well as investments in lumber and mining operations.

The family history is that my great-grandfather, a drunk, pissed away a large portion of the fortune, but there was still a bit left as it passed down to my grandfather. The money didn't exactly make for family stability though. My dad's father was never around, and his mother loved her kids, but was pretty unstable and while she was there physically, mentally she was far away.

My dad and his three brothers were raised by their German nanny. Nothing says warmth and empathy quite like a German nanny. No surprise that he was always in trouble and pretty well known to the authorities in the area as he was growing up. He had an anti-authority streak then that lasts to this day.

My mother, Susanne, on the other hand, couldn't be more different. When someone thought up the saying, "opposites attract," they were thinking of my parents. She's from Hässleholm, Sweden, but spent many summers in Åhus, a seaside resort town located in Skåne County on the east coast of the country. It's a beautiful town that dates back to the 11th century. In addition to all the architectural attractions you'd expect in an old European town, it's home to Absolut, the vodka distiller. That probably draws as many tourists as all the cultural attractions.

Many of my mom's relatives still live there, and because they're obviously mine too, I'm lucky enough to be able to go and visit in the summer and spend time with them. Even though many of my older relatives don't speak English, and my Swedish is pretty basic at best, we find a way to understand each other. Blood is thicker than water, after all.

My mom came to the States as an au pair and met my dad dancing at a nightclub in Fort Lauderdale, where he had moved after school. The quiet, sweet, some might say naive, Swedish woman and the brash, opinionated American guy, who was teaching dancing and apparently had quite the moves, hit it off.

She never moved back to Sweden. They married in Pittsburgh, moved to Michigan and became parents when my older brother Robbie was born in 1985. I came four years after my brother, who was and is as good a big brother as any kid could ask for. I've looked up to him since as long as I can remember.

We lived in a nice big house with a big yard surrounded by woods. My brother and I were always outside, no matter the season. It wasn't that we were forced to or would face a list of chores if we didn't. We just had a lot of energy and it's a lot easier to burn it off running loose outside than it is staying cooped up indoors.

Between the two of us, we had loads of friends, and my childhood was a blur of activity—running through the woods playing war games, pick-up football games year-round, whizzing through the neighborhood on bicycles, sledding, street hockey—anything that kept us moving was fair game. But it was ice hockey that really grabbed our interest. My brother was a good player and I wanted to emulate him, so from the age of six until I graduated high school, I was on the ice almost daily.

After four years of hockey and as little schoolwork as I could get away with at Pioneer High School, which is across the street from the Michigan Wolverines' 107,601-seat Big House football stadium, I decided to attend Eastern Michigan University just outside Detroit to play club hockey for two ex-NHL players turned coaches.

They were legendary Detroit Red Wing, Lee Norwood, and University of Michigan star, Billy Muckalt. Norwood had a 12-year NHL career, while Muckalt played six years. Given his reputation as a hard-nosed defenseman who earned the nickname "Hack" (Gilbert Delorme, his defensive partner on the Red Wings, was nicknamed "Whack") it should have been no surprise that Lee was a tough son of a bitch to play for.

"I've spilled more fucking Jack than you pussies have ever drank combined," Lee used to yell at the 25 of us sitting in the locker room. It was hard to know whether we should smirk or hide.

Fortunately, Billy's slightly softer touch kept us from being too scared to come to the rink. Their life experience playing in the NHL in the 1990s and early 2000s produced lots of great stories and motivational speeches.

Besides hockey, I studied partying and film at Eastern Michigan University, which frankly, wasn't exactly a hotbed for film making, either then or now. The partying was a different story. I excelled at that, but the film making didn't end up being my calling.

I did direct a couple of films though, including a documentary about a local boxer who fought former WBU light-welterweight champ Mickey Ward, before his girlfriend's death and his addictions sent him in a downward spiral that had him homeless and on the streets. It had potential, but due to his erratic schedule and lack of communication I wasn't able to finish the film. Between that and a few student films, I graduated with a listing on the IMDb website as a director, so I have that as a souvenir of my filmmaking career.

During my four-year career at Eastern, I lived in the Hockey House with many other players on the team. It's safe to say we had a good time living on Ypsilanti's infamous "Normal Street," where the fraternities and sports team houses were situated.

Even though we lived in the center of the action, I often found myself meandering down the hill to Ballard Street to attend the school's Reserve Officers' Training Corps (ROTC) cadet parties. These days, I'm much more likely to send an ROTC cadet out to the motor pool to do chores to get rid of them, but back then I enjoyed their company, and I was thankful for the service they pledged to our country.

In the blink of an eye, it was over. It was time to enter the real world of work and responsibility. With a useless diploma in hand and in search of new beginnings, I moved out to Huntington Beach, California, over two thousand miles and countless ocean sunsets away from the cold Michigan winters. I managed to get a good paying job, a condo on the beach, a brand new cherry-red Ford F-150, and I got to surf every day, which in itself is pretty mind-blowing for a guy who grew up in the Midwest.

Things couldn't be better. So why, at the age of 27, was I feeling a magnetic pull to join the military?

The short version of that answer is that I missed being part of a team. Even though I was working for a great company, I was on my own most of the time. While I had developed a circle of friends in Huntington Beach, I missed the close brotherhood feeling I got from playing hockey all those years. But I was past my prime and the prospects of playing in anything other than a recreation league were in the rear view mirror.

Anyone who's played the game knows that the connection you develop with your hockey teammates is pretty special. It's a game that relies on teamwork and having each other's back, no matter what. I missed that, and I only knew of one place where I thought I might find that same tight-knit sense of community.

The longer answer is that for as far back as I can remember, I was drawn to military life. As a kid, I'd find myself studying the classic Navy SEAL poster my brother had on his wall just above the TV we played original PlayStation games on. I'd also perk up whenever one of those iconic 2000-era Army commercials came on the TV. One stands out vividly in my mind: the Army theme song plays in the background to a symphony of gunfire and RPG blasts, while helo blades swirling in the air kick up a cloud of dust on some distant battleground. Through the dust, a squad of soldiers appear running towards the gunfire. A deep, bass voice asks, "Which way would you run?"

I remember thinking about which way I would run. I thought how great it would be to one day get to make that decision, I daydreamed about what it would be like to step foot out of a helo and onto the dusty Afghan soil.

But while I did, I was very much aware of the fact that my parents wouldn't approve of a military career for one of their sons. Growing up in a financially comfortable family in Ann Arbor, I certainly wasn't in a position where the military was my best option to get ahead in life. Whenever I would see a uniformed service member, I would think, why should they serve, but not me? Even back then, I was fully aware that our enlisted military is made up of young working-class men and women. That never seemed right to me.

Combined with the fact that my family had no military background, my interest in joining seemed odd to the very few people I ever told this aspiration to. So, for the longest time, I ignored it. But the dream of enlisting and serving lingered in my blood like a powerful drug. At the age of 27, I finally gave in to it. I began sifting through information about the different service branches and quickly determined that the Air Force didn't really interest me, and there was no way I was going to wear one of those white Navy uniforms.

That left two real options for me (sorry Coast Guard). It would be the Marines or the Army. I called the recruiters, who were both located in the same building in the Huntington Beach recruiting office. Both informed me that since I had a bachelor's degree, I had the option of going in as either an officer or enlisted. I decided pretty early on that even though the officer route made more money and arguably earned more respect, I didn't want to be pushing paper. I wanted to be in the field directly involved in the mission.

After talking it over with both recruiters, the decision was made easy. Since I had my degree, the Army was going to let me start at the rank of E-4, which was a specialist, while the Marines were still going to make me start as a private. Apparently the crayon-eating Marines don't care about an education!

All jokes aside, I learned that Marines are typically very squared away and it was always a pleasure anytime we got to work with them. They are members of a special institution and they know it. Their attitude is well earned and it's always commanded my respect. But given the choice of starting on the bottom rung, or in the middle of the ladder, I opted for the higher perch.

So the Army it was. Now to tell my family.

I had to fly across the country to New York that following weekend for my brother's surprise proposal to his then girlfriend, now lovely wife, Mackenzie. After an amazing weekend celebrating their future together, I found some time alone with my father as we walked down a Brooklyn street. It seemed like the right time to tell him about my plans. Though he was completely caught off guard by the news, he told me it was very admirable, and I had his support. That meant a lot to me then, and it still does now.

Shortly after, I made the move back to Michigan and picked up with a local Army recruiter on the east side of town. I walked into the office unannounced and ended up sitting at the desk of Sergeant First Class Kott. I was not his average customer. With a prospective recruit who was approaching 30 years old and making a six-figure income at his day job sitting in front of him, I could tell he was surprised to see me there. I definitely didn't fit the profile of an average Army recruit.

But we got down to business, and went through the different jobs available to me. I finally decided to become an engineer. With my building industry sales background and my family's involvement building custom homes, it was the right fit. Plus, it was a respectable job in the Army, and it would get me out into the field. I wouldn't be jumping out of helos into a raging firefight, but then, I wasn't a wide-eyed teenager anymore either.

I signed on the dotted line that day. About a month later I went into MEPS (Military Entrance Processing Station) to get sworn in. Fort Benning, Georgia, here I come.

CHAPTER 3

Basic Training

My report day for basic training was February 22, 2017. My recruiter dropped me off at the McNamara terminal at Detroit Metro to get on my Delta flight direct to Atlanta. I fly a lot for my job these days, and every time I walk through that terminal I remember how nervous I was to get on the plane that day.

I stepped off the plane in Atlanta and opened up my manila envelope to look at the next set of instructions. "Head to the clock tower in the Atrium and await pickup," it read. When I got there, a line had already formed of new recruits standing nervously silent at attention.

That was the first time I saw a dreaded drill sergeant (DS) in person. There's something about a DS that's just terrifying. Even today I can't be perfectly comfortable around them, even though I outranked many of them by the time I finished my enlistment.

Anyone who's ever been through basic training in any branch of the military can tell you it's an alternate reality to the world you've left behind. Most people who are unfamiliar with military basic training think of it as a physical endurance test. But anyone who's been through it knows it's a reality-bending mental mind fuck masquerading as a character-building exercise. Where else can grown men act as sadistically insane as a DS and not get arrested?

We boarded a bus to Fort Benning at 8:00 p.m. and pulled up to the 30th Adjutant General Battalion reception building around 10:00 p.m. When the bus stopped, all eyes locked on a DS as he made his way over.

I couldn't even tell you what he said because my nerves were going 100mph. I do remember him eventually yelling, "Get off my bus." Of course, I shot to my feet and quickly exited the bus, but it wasn't more than a few seconds before I found myself in the "front leaning rest position," which is military jargon for doing pushups. I found myself in that position a lot. It's the default DS command when they can't think of anything else to scream at you.

We spent the whole night in processing, getting the clothing and gear needed to complete training. At around 7:00 a.m. they finally escorted us to the barracks to get our assigned bunks. I was exhausted and ready to get some sleep. "Throw your gear on your bunk and get outside! You have 30 seconds!" I should have seen that coming. The Army day was already in full swing, and they weren't going to let us mess up that schedule. Time to adapt.

After a tortuously slow day that seemed like it would never end, I was ready to curl up and sleep anywhere. I would have been happy with a bed made of nails. Unfortunately, some of the guys in the barracks had different plans. As soon as the lights went out, one of them jumped up and challenged everyone in the room to a fight. He started jumping on bunks throwing haymakers. An all-out fight erupted as I sat on my bunk. I've never been to prison but this is what I imagine it to be like. It was no surprise that a soldier tried to run away that night. Not quite sure what his plan was, but he only made it a couple miles before getting picked up by the MPs.

After reception, we loaded the buses and headed to my new home, Alpha Company, 2nd Battalion, 47th Infantry Regiment. The unit had a long history of fighting wars dating back to World War I. It was also the unit Forrest Gump deployed with to Vietnam in the fictional movie. Unlike Forrest, I couldn't run out the front door and keep on going. This was real life.

The bus pulled up to our barracks, where our unit's drill sergeants were waiting. It was time for the infamous shark attack. The next few hours involved being chased from bus to buildings by a variety of DSs as they screamed full blast and sprayed spit in our ears, accompanied by an exercise known as bag drills.

It didn't take long to find out that holding your 60lb gear bag above your head for 30 continuous minutes is impossible. When you inevitably dropped it, more fun exercises followed. The sense that I might have made a mistake coming here began kicking in hard at this point.

It wouldn't be the last time. One story in particular is too good not to share. It was the end of week one. I was in 1st Platoon, the "Rough Riders," but it was common for the DSs from the other platoons to come mess with us for some reason. They apparently enjoyed watching us suffer. Did I mention the word "sadistic?"

One night a DS from 2nd Platoon nicknamed "Tsunami" came into our bay. He was from the Pacific Islands and was an absolutely terrifying human being. To this day, if I saw him I'd jump straight to parade rest (the position you stand at with your arms behind your back when a non-commissioned officer is speaking to you).

Following him were the rest of the DSs from the company. "Toe the line!" he shouted at the top of his lungs. This is a command to stand on the line at the edge of your bunk. In the middle of every barracks there is what is known as the "kill zone." You're not allowed to step into the kill zone for any reason. If you need to cross the room, you need to walk all the way to the end of the barracks and around the kill zone.

When we were lined up, Tsunami told us to go fill up our camel packs with water and return to the bay. We did. "Dump it on your head," he instructed. We blindly obeyed, as was expected. So began a four-hour smoke session of us doing pushups in our bay, while the DS went into the bathroom and clogged up the showers and the sinks while running the water.

The room began filling with water. By the second hour it was up to our ankles. By hour three, it was much deeper and the DSs had us practicing our swim strokes. "Breast stroke!" they would call out, followed by "Back stroke!"

At one point I woke up from a minor blackout with my head under water. *This is so fucked up*, I thought to myself. After the swim drills were completed at hour four, they allowed us to get up. But we weren't done yet. They made us go to our locker and grab a picture of our loved ones if we had one. We then stood in a circle holding up the pictures as a few members of the platoon were forced to go around the circle, look you in the eye and say "Fuck your [insert family member]."

It was a test to see who was loyal to the platoon. We were so brain dead that almost everyone failed. By that point, we were all crying our eyes out, a bunch of pitiful grown men soaked and sobbing. They had officially broken us.

As a reward, they made us clean up the bay and head to bed. That same night at 2:00 a.m. they came sprinting in the bay with a manila envelope, I remember them waving it around and telling us that a U.S. submarine had just fired a missile at and destroyed a Russian vessel.

"World War III is on, privates!" one of them yelled. We all stared at each other in disbelief. "We have to train, privates!" they yelled. We all jumped out of bed and down to the PT field to get some more exercise in. We were motivated as hell that morning.

Looking back it's comical to think we actually believed them. But at Fort Benning, the DSs are like God. You believe everything they say, and without access to phones or the outside world, you have no way to fact check anything anyway.

Throughout my 10 weeks at basic I ended up losing 25 pounds, coming in at 205 and leaving at 180. The constant exercise, stress, no booze or junk food all contributed to the loss. In addition to being a great weight-loss program, basic was a friendship incubator. I met some amazing guys there. While I don't talk to these old friends often, I know if I ever run into them, we'll share a big hug and a lot of stories. Hope you boys are doing well.

By the end, I stood tall in my dress blues and walked across the parade field as a soldier. After another eight weeks in Mississippi for Army Engineer school, I reported back home to my assigned unit in Toledo, Ohio.

CHAPTER 4

Deployment

I reported to my unit—486th Engineer Company of the 983rd Engineer Battalion—a few weeks later. Luckily, there were a couple familiar faces of guys that had gone through training with me. The unit is based in Monclova, in northwest Ohio, just outside the city of Toledo.

The 486th had originally been activated in 1942 and served in northern France during World War II. After the war, it had been activated, inactivated, and moved around a number of times, before finally being activated in Monclova in 2008. That's eventually where I settled in and cruised through the first two years of my enlistment.

In early 2019, I made the 75-mile ride down from my house for a routine weekend formation. Just prior to falling in, I overheard one soldier saying to another, "Did you hear the news? We're deploying."

I had been in long enough to not get too excited about hearing this. The PNN (Private News Network) rumor hotline is the fastest-moving source of information anywhere in the United States. With an accuracy rating of around 10 percent, the PNN is capable of sending incorrect military information across the country in the time it takes to send a text.

But like the saying goes, a stopped clock is right twice a day. This time, the PNN had the real scoop. After we formed up, our first sergeant made the announcement that we were being looked at for an upcoming deployment. The destination wasn't certain, but they knew it was in the Middle East, he said.

As you can imagine, the news sparked a weekend of excited talk about where we might be going. Some guys wanted Iraq, some Syria, a few wanted to just live it up in the upscale bases of Kuwait and sunbathe in the desert for a year.

Me, I wanted Afghanistan. I had always been fascinated with the culture and the formidable terrain that had helped defeat every foreign army that ever invaded. The list of failed invaders is long and noteworthy. It includes Alexander the Great, Genghis Khan, the British, the Soviets, and most recently us and the NATO forces who had been there for the last 18 years. Of course, I had no way of knowing that we would be some of the last troops to enter Afghanistan.

As American politicians started planning the best way to quietly lose the war like invaders past, we started preparing for deployment. Even then though, the government knew something we didn't. There was already talk about a full U.S. withdrawal. The dream of a westernized Afghanistan was never going to happen.

Nonetheless, the attitude at the unit changed. New soldiers slotted in from sister units to fill empty spots and the training got more serious. One of the new soldiers to join my platoon was Sergeant Garrett Viars, and I knew instantly that we were going to be friends. He was one of the guys who joined the Army because he wanted to, not because he had to.

There's a distinct difference between those two. The Army tends to attract people who enlist just for the benefits, or high-school dropouts who can't find work. While many of them end up being good soldiers, some are what we refer to as "Shitbags." It's inevitable in any large organization. And like any other large organization, the Army is better off without them.

On the other hand, the guys who join because they want to are almost always squared away. That was Viars. The only thing I hated about him was that he was an Ohio State Buckeye. As an Ann Arbor, Michigan native and die hard Wolverines fan, this was like making friends with the enemy.

Viars and I were in 1st Platoon, whose call sign was "Beaver." We loved the innuendo that came along with the name. It pushed the limits just far enough where you might get an eye squint, but not enough that you get called out for it. After all, we were engineers; building was our specialty. Since I was the Alpha Team Leader in 1st Squad, my call sign was "Beaver One Alpha." I'm going to go out on a limb and say this may be one of the best call signs in military history.

Towards the end of the summer we finally got confirmation about our final destination. I felt like a lottery winner when our platoon sergeant came storming into our barracks after a team meeting with the news that we were headed to Afghanistan.

When the shouting calmed down, he said our final destination would be a small camp in northern Afghanistan. Which, he added, "receives a shit ton of IDF [indirect fire]." Apparently the Taliban liked to take potshots at the base with mortars, he explained.

For the first time, my excitement about being deployed edged slightly into fear territory. It's not a TV commercial or video game, I thought. This is actually happening.

Luckily that feeling only lasted until the next morning. I calmed myself by thinking about this Marcus Aurelius quote, "Never let the future disturb you. You will meet it, if you have to, with the same weapons of reason which today arm you against the present." I thought to myself, the time for fear may come, but it's not now.

I headed out to the PT field. I remember watching the sun rise over the mountains behind the flagpole. We all took a minute to take it in. Viars broke the silence. "If you're needing any motivation today, remember that eighteen years ago, three thousand people died just trying to go to work. That's why we're here." Everyone nodded and got to work. It was September 11.

On November 17, 2019, after a blistering hot, mind-numbing month at Camp Buehring in Kuwait and a dizzying combat descent on the C-17 as it approached Bagram Air Base, we touched down in Afghanistan. It was dark and refreshingly cold after the Kuwait heat. Two fighter jets screamed past us as we walked off the tarmac. Every nerve-ending in my body felt alive.

I fell asleep to the sounds of outgoing fire, and in the morning, I stepped outside the barracks to scan the incredible landscape that ringed the airfield. The treacherously steep snow-capped mountains were the most beautiful sight I'd ever seen. I was instantly in love with the country.

After a week of trying to find my way around the giant airfield, staring in awe at the mountains, and keeping an ear and eye peeled for the IDF alarm and the designated bunkers, I got my orders to manifest on a C-130 flight to Mazar-e Sharif (MES) to report to Camp Marmal, a German-run NATO base on the southern outskirts of the northern Afghanistan city.

Bagram was on high alert the day we left. The night before, a U.S. Apache attack helicopter had crashed seven miles from the base while it was providing ground support, and it was still unknown whether the Taliban had shot it down or not. As it turns out, one of the two U.S. pilots who died in the crash, Chief Warrant Officer 2 Kirk Fuchigami Jr., went to flight school with a guy in my basic training unit at Fort Benning. It was a solemn reminder that Afghanistan remained a dangerous place.

MES is located in the far north of the country, just 35 miles from the border with Uzbekistan. With a population of 600,000, it's Afghanistan's fourth-largest city and is considered an important and strategically located regional capital. It sits at the base of the Hindu Kush mountains at an elevation of only 1,100 feet, which makes the nearby towering mountains appear even taller than the ones that ring Bagram. It's a spectacularly beautiful part of the world.

Mazar-e Sharif and the outlying Balkh Province had been spared the heavy fighting and damage that had leveled so many other areas of the country. Most of the fighting up north happened early in the war. But the Taliban presence and the fear they injected into the Afghan population always lurked in the region.

In 2018, dozens of Afghans who worked as interpreters, security guards and kitchen help at the camp blocked the main gate in protest against the German government's refusal to grant them political asylum after promising to do so. The Taliban had threatened them and their families, they said, and they feared for their lives.

At Camp Marmal we had a small U.S. presence that mainly consisted of U.S. Special Forces, an ODA team (Operational Detachment Alpha), and their support staff. As engineers, our mission at Marmal was to construct barracks huts, "B Huts" for short, for future incoming troops.

Camp Marmal is located at nearly the exact spot where the true story and follow-up Hollywood movie, *12 Strong*, took place. The movie tells the amazing story of ODA 595 riding through the Hindu Kush mountains and the Tangi pass on horseback in October 2001 with the mission of taking the city of Mazar-e Sharif back from the Taliban.

The 12 Green Beret soldiers of ODA 595, also known as the "Horse Soldiers," were the first American troops in Afghanistan. They were there to support what was left of the Northern Alliance after the coordinated assassination of its leader, Ahmad Shah Massoud, at the hands of Al-Qaeda just two days before the 9/11 attacks.

Teaming up with the infamous Uzbek warlord General Dostum, ODA 595 and its Afghan allies thundered through the mountain passes, took MES, and sent Taliban and Al-Qaeda forces backpedaling in full retreat. Many analysts suspected this could take up to two years to accomplish. ODA 595 did it in three weeks.

There's a monument commemorating the bravery of these guys outside the gates of Camp Marmal. I spent many evenings staring at the pass through the mountains wondering what that experience would have been like.

Compared to the combat outposts that so many of our troops spent time in during our 20 years in Afghanistan, Camp Marmal offered a pretty cushy lifestyle. The Germans definitely knew how to do deployment in style. So did all the other NATO countries who rotated troops in during the 15 years it was open. The espresso machines and breakfast pastries kept me motivated to arrive to chow on time. If I got tired of hanging with Americans, I could go to the cigar club and light up with soldiers from Norway, Croatia, Sweden, even Georgia and Mongolia. The international flavor of the camp made the deployment feel even more foreign and it definitely made it more interesting.

But it wasn't all fun and games for me there. Camp Marmal's laid-back atmosphere also allowed me time in the evening to pursue a master's degree. I would work during the day, then at night when everyone was playing video games or watching movies, I would hit the books. A free MBA funded by the Army was just too good to pass up.

Just up the hill from our barracks was a small bazaar where all the local Afghans and interpreters gathered to eat, drink tea and talk.

It was there where the story really begins. There, in that fairly nondescript little area thousands of miles from my home, my life intersected with Abdul and Mohammad's lives, and the path led us to the place we're all at today.

The engineer unit we were replacing was headed back to the States. Before they left, one of their staff sergeants took me on a tour of the base. We ended up at the bazaar, where he introduced me to a bearded Afghan wearing a traditional white outfit.

"I can vouch for this man. He's a good man and he'll get you whatever you need for your mission," he told me. It was Mohammad. He smiled and greeted me, and then introduced me to the man standing next to him. His brother-in-law, Abdul.

After we all exchanged greetings, I turned to leave, but Mohammad stopped me and handed me a black scarf. "Please," he said, "It's our gift, welcome to Afghanistan." It was my introduction to the legendary hospitality of Afghans. Little did I know, it wouldn't be the last time with these two guys.

Over the next two months I developed a friendship with Mohammad and Abdul. I was fascinated with Afghanistan and would stop by to see them in my free time and pepper them with questions about their country and culture. They were always patient and good-natured and, despite our cultural differences, we laughed easily together.

From time to time they would show up at our job site with a home-cooked meal of lamb kabobs and naan bread, which was a favorite of all the guys in the platoon—and a meal I still would run through a hail of bullets to get.

They also proved themselves very useful getting anything we needed for our engineering missions. Using our military pipeline for supplies could take forever, so whenever we could, we would ask Mohammad and Abdul to acquire materials for us. They were happy to do so, and could do it in half the time the military could.

Sometimes they would both make their way over to our project to see if they could take any spare lumber we had laying around, which they would use to heat their homes and donate to their neighbors as well.

The sharp contrasts in our lifestyles were hard to ignore. After talking with them, I often thought about how much we take for granted growing up in the U.S. Sure, we have our own problems, but most of us don't have to worry about whether we'll have enough food, shelter, heat and other basic necessities. Those were constant worries for the average Afghan then, and unfortunately, even more so now.

I often joked with Abdul that he would need to come visit me in Michigan once I got home. He would get a wistful look on his face and reply by saying it was his dream to see the United States one day. It's funny how conversations that don't have much significance at the time can seem so prophetic and meaningful when you look back at them later on.

The time went by way too quickly. In what seemed like the blink of an eye, we finished up our assignment and prepared to be rotated out to the next one. It was late January when I found Mohammad and Abdul on base and delivered the news that I would be leaving. We shared a hug, exchanged WhatsApp phone numbers and they surprised me with a custom traditional Afghan outfit. They were the most generous, resilient and unassuming men I had ever met. I would miss them.

As I said goodbye, it was with the unspoken understanding that this would almost surely be the last time we'd see each other face to face. Despite our friendship and the banter about them coming to visit me in the States, there didn't seem to be any likely scenario in which that would happen. It was a bittersweet goodbye, but I made sure to hold a smile for our last handshake.

We made our way from Marmal to Camp Morehead for the remainder of the deployment. I jumped out of the helicopter into the rotor wash from the circling blades and took in my new surroundings. Dug into the side of a mountain on the south side of Kabul, Camp Morehead was occupied by a small presence of U.S. and NATO Special Forces, a platoon of 10th Mountain Infantry, and our platoon of engineers.

It was a small camp that was attached to the Afghan National Army (ANA) Commando training unit. Most of our Special Operations Forces were there to train the ANA commandos up to U.S. standards. While I enjoyed the relaxed vibe of being deployed to a Special Operations camp, where uniform and grooming regulations didn't exist, I missed my friends, Abdul and Mohammad.

In February 2020, we heard about President Trump's peace talks with the Taliban to end America's longest war. So did our Afghan allies. I sensed an uneasiness among them. Habibi, a new Afghan friend I made at Morehead, asked me if we would be leaving soon.

"Not sure," I replied. "Please don't leave sir," he begged, as if I actually had the power to make that decision. "If you leave, we will all be killed for working with you."

Looking back on this now, it is very obvious to me that the real message we sent to the Taliban during those negotiations was, "You win. As soon as we leave, you can take over and do what you want." That's definitely how Habibi, Abdul, Mohammad and the rest of our allies saw it.

That's the moment we should have been expediting visas and coordinating evacuation of the tens of thousands of Afghans who stood side by side with us. But instead the president did nothing, and then the next president did nothing but blame the previous president. Both of them were oblivious to the code of honor in the military community: you don't ever leave anyone behind. But what can you expect when you elect people who do everything they can to avoid serving their own country?

June came and U.S. bases were closing down all over the country. My deployment was over and it was time for me to leave Afghanistan. I got on a helicopter out of Camp Morehead and headed back to Bagram Air Base to catch a flight. On this visit, Bagram was a ghost town. The base that held 100,000 troops in 2012 now only hosted several thousand.

I took one last look at the towering mountains, pulled in one last gulp of Afghan air, then trudged into the C-17 to start the long journey home.

As cushy as the deployment was, military suicide statistics don't lie, nor discriminate. During our 10-month deployment, three soldiers in my platoon became suicidal. Thankfully, they were able to get help or were medevac'd out. Three out of 30, 10 percent, and none of them even saw combat. I'm thankful that at this moment, they're all still alive. I also know that as a military community, we have a long way to go when it comes to combating mental health.

As for me, I was glad to be home. I caught up on missed time with my family and my girlfriend, Ashlynn. But Afghanistan was never far from my mind. It was hard to listen to the news and hear reports about Taliban advances. The people and the country had made an indelible impression on me.

As the battles between the Taliban and the Afghan government raged on, all I could do from a distance was to stay in touch with Abdul via WhatsApp to make sure they were unharmed. It was a powerless feeling.

How was I to know how much power a phone connection and a message app could have? Just over a year later, I would find out.

CHAPTER 5

A Kabul Childhood

Abdul and Mohammad grew up together in a residential neighborhood in the sprawling Afghan capital of Kabul. Like most Kabul homes, theirs were modest and jam-packed with their large families. Mohammad, who's the older of the two by just under three years, lived with his mother, father, three brothers and five sisters. Abdul, his parents, and his three brothers and four sisters lived nearby.

Needless to say, most of us Americans can't even wrap our brains around living in such crowded conditions. Or living with so many family members. Many of us struggle to make it through Thanksgiving Day together.

I'm also sure few of us could imagine growing up in a city that has endured so much pain and suffering in just their short lifetimes.

Home to 4.6 million people now, the city sits at an elevation of over a mile high in a valley between the jagged peaks of the Hindu Kush mountain range. Situated at a halfway point between Istanbul and Hanoi, Kabul has always been a key stop on trade routes between Asia and Europe, which has made it a coveted prize for the war-mongering conquerors I mentioned earlier.

Mohammad was born in July 1988, just a few months before the Soviet Army withdrew from Afghanistan after their 10-year occupation. After killing over a million Afghans and committing documented atrocities against the civilian population,[1] the Soviets licked their wounds and withdrew in February 1989.

---

1   Human Rights Watch website, www.hrw.org, 7/6/05.

Their plan on coming in for a year (following the tried-and-true Russian playbook of saying they were invited by the host country) to stabilize a Communist government and show the loose collection of militias and warlords opposed to them who was boss, had gone badly off the rails. As they're demonstrating in Ukraine now, Russia's geopolitical goals are one thing, but their understanding of the reality on the ground is very different. They completely underestimated the strength of the opposition, the difficulty of the terrain and the weather.

Instead of learning and adapting, they resorted to brute force, as the NGO Human Rights Watch documented in a 2005 report. The more the Mujahideen fighters fought back, the more brutal the Soviet tactics became. During the course of the war, they resorted to indiscriminate shelling and air strikes, "depopulation tactics" in Pashtun areas, torture and systemic rape.

Most of that brutality took place in the countryside in southern and eastern regions, where a majority of the Pashtun opposition fighters were based. Aside from a few acts of violence over the 10-year occupation, Kabul escaped relatively unharmed.

The Mujahideen fighters who eventually bloodied the Soviets and sent them back to where they came were battle-hardened and emboldened by their success. Some of them eventually laid down arms and became government ministers years later. Others, like Osama bin Laden, took the experience and knowledge gained and looked beyond the country's borders for a new enemy to fight.

Many others, though, did what warlords do and turned on each other.

When Abdul was born in March 1991, Kabul still remained relatively calm. The pro-Soviet government of President Mohammed Najibullah had surprisingly managed to fight off the factions of Mujahideen without Soviet military support.

Their individual thirst for power made that job much easier. Made up of an "alliance" of seven major warlords with their own militias, the Mujahideen soon became too busy fighting each other to gain territorial control and military assets to unify against their common enemy. They had stuck together against the Russian invaders, but the facade of unity vanished when the Soviets left.

Najibullah managed to stave them off for another year, but his government was abandoned by the Soviets as their own political system unraveled for the world to see. The new Russian government under Boris Yeltsin decided to stop supplying Najibullah with oil, which signaled his end. Isolated and surrounded by the shifting alliances of warlords who smelled blood in the water, he stepped down in April 1992.

Abdul had just turned a year old. Mohammad would turn four in three months. In their short lives, they had lived through more political turmoil than most Westerners see in a lifetime. Unfortunately for them, their families, and the residents of Kabul, it was just the beginning.

In talking to them both about their childhoods, neither one brings up the war-torn atmosphere where they spent their young lives. They'll answer direct questions about their feelings about the Taliban, and they'll talk about the fear that Kabul residents felt as they closed in on the capital in July 2021, but with just one- or two-word answers.

Part of that is a language thing. Their English is passable and it's improving, but it's difficult for them to find the words to express emotion. I suppose that's natural for anyone not speaking in their native tongue. But I also think it's a default survival mechanism for most Afghans. When you come from a country where war is a way of life and its people are scattered in refugee camps around the globe, you have to be able to put the past behind you and focus on the present in order to survive. Theirs is a pragmatic "mindfulness." They are the most resilient people I have ever met.

For these guys, now in Michigan, they're adapting to a completely new way of life—finding jobs, learning the language, paying bills, helping their children adjust to school. Most of their family is stuck back in Kabul living in a virtual prison created by the Taliban. And yet, they hardly talk about it, although I know it weighs heavily on them.

Back in Kabul in 1992, Najibullah tried to hightail it to India, but he was cut off by a warlord's troops at the Kabul Airport, and ended up seeking refuge with his brother in the United Nations compound in Kabul. He stayed there for nearly four years.

In the meantime, the warlords went haywire trying to seize control of Kabul for themselves. Eleven armed groups vied for the city. In four years of what can only be called pure insanity, they killed thousands of Kabul civilians by firing artillery and rockets into crowded residential neighborhoods with absolutely no military value.

For all the sadistic tactics that the Russians practiced in Afghanistan, the warlords took it to another level. War between foreign adversaries is horrible. Civil war is barbaric and impossible for any rational human to understand.

BBC correspondent, Jeremy Bowen, said later, "Before it started, Kabul was very much intact. It was surprising how intact it was. Afterwards, of course, it was completely destroyed."

This internecine violence created a perfect vacuum for the Taliban to form and rapidly expand. Born in 1994 in the Islamic schools of Pakistan and the rural regions of eastern and southern Afghanistan, the Taliban (which means "students" or "seekers" in Pashto) and its strict interpretation of Sharia law grew rapidly under the leadership of Mohammed Omar Mujahid and with the support of Pakistan and its powerful intelligence service, ISI.

As the warlords battled over Kabul, the Taliban swept through large swaths of the rest of the country, seizing Kandahar in 1994 and Herat in 1995. In early September, 1996, they took Jalalabad and arrived at the outskirts of Kabul. Even though they had named Kandahar as their capital, Kabul remained the big prize.

Much to the surprise of everyone, they strolled into the city on September 27, 1996 with barely any opposition. In fact, it was so eerily quiet, Taliban leaders thought it was a trap. Instead, it was an indication of the fear Kabul's residents had of their arrival. The roads leading north and west out of the city were choked with people fleeing with anything they could carry.

Seeing they had no battles to fight for the moment, Kabul's new conquerors' first order of business was to storm the United Nations compound, drag out ex-President Najibullah and his brother, torture them, castrate them, and then hang them from a streetlight. Where they stayed for two days: a chilling message to the residents who were too poor or sick or old to flee.

The reason why they barely had to break a sweat to take the city was that Ahmad Shah Massoud, the leader of the Northern Alliance, had assessed the battlefield and decided a withdrawal would let him live to fight another day. Nicknamed "The Lion of Panjshir," Massoud had emerged from the war against the Soviets as one of the country's most feared and respected fighters and leaders. He was appointed minister of defense in the post-Communist government, and was so respected by the Taliban that they repeatedly asked him to take the prime minister position when they seized control. A perfect example of the adage, "Keep your friends close and your enemies closer."

But he was fundamentally opposed to their interpretation of Islam, especially their subjugation of women, so he refused. After five years of battling Massoud following their takeover, the Taliban's terrorist client, Al-Qaeda, managed to do what the Soviets, Pakistanis and the Taliban could not: they killed him when a suicide bomber sent by Bin Laden detonated an explosive concealed in a video camera. The bomber was posing as a documentary film maker. It happened on September 9, 2001.

It was a short-lived win for Bin Laden. Instead of disintegrating with the loss of their leader, Massoud's Northern Alliance fighters teamed up with U.S. Special Forces and CIA covert operations teams to corner him and nearly kill him in the caves of Bora Bora. It didn't work out so well for the Taliban either, because Bin Laden brought the wrath of the United States down on Afghanistan and ended the Taliban's brutal rule for the next 20 years.

Researching and writing this short summary of war, bloodshed and shifting alliances in Afghanistan is like peeling back the skin of an onion; one layer after another, but no core, no center, nothing solid to hold on to. It's no wonder invading armies throughout history stagger out of Afghanistan licking their wounds.

I recently watched a short YouTube video shot in 2001 in Kabul after the Taliban had been forced to flee and the Northern Alliance troops had entered the city. The streets were packed with smiling, ecstatic residents. They were tasting freedom for the first time in years and they were drunk with happiness.

There were long lines of people waiting to get into the reopened movie cinemas. Street vendors were selling TVs and VCRs, movies and music, all banned under the Taliban. Other vendors set up tables overflowing with formerly banned items, including soccer balls and chess sets.

But the best scene was the one showing Afghan kids flying kites. It's a favorite pastime of Afghan youngsters—and the adults they grow up to become. Actually, it's more accurate to call it a way of life than a pastime. Like so many things that are considered "fun," it was banned under the Taliban. The few kids brave enough to defy the ban were beaten, and some imprisoned.

Any of those happy, smiling children in the video could have been Mohammad or Abdul or their brothers or sisters for all I know. They would have been 13 and 10 at the time. I'll have to watch it with them some day and see if they spot themselves.

But not now. Maybe I'll need to save that for the next time the Taliban are driven out of Kabul. It would depress them to see that with their family still there, and it would remind them that there are kids there now who still want nothing more than to fly a goddamned kite.

CHAPTER 6

Early Summer 2021

The hourglass that measured America's 20-year war in Afghanistan was almost completely filled. The ink on the Doha Agreement, signed by the Trump administration with the Taliban in Qatar in February 2020 agreeing to a complete U.S. withdrawal, was dry and the curtain was set to come down.

In April 2021, President Biden formally announced that his administration would honor the agreement. After nearly 2,400 KIA, 20,000 wounded and $2 trillion in expenditure, we were on our way out. Now it was time to execute the withdrawal.

For the Pentagon brass in charge of doing that, it meant overlooking the fact that their advice to keep 2,500 U.S. troops in the country to prevent an Al-Qaeda resurgence had been rejected by the Biden administration. In the line of U.S. presidents embroiled in Afghanistan that stretched from Bush to Obama to Trump to him, Biden decided to ignore the advice of his leading military advisers. It wasn't a popular decision in the military community.

General Frank McKenzie, head of U.S. Central Command, said as much later in an August, 2022 interview with Voice of America. One year after the Kabul evacuation, the now-retired McKenzie suggested that a force that size could have maintained control of the massive Bagram Air Base 25 miles north of Kabul and worked with the Afghan National Army and allies to prevent Al-Qaeda from regaining a foothold in the country.

He also said that he believed the decision to shut the Afghan government out of the Doha talks with the Taliban was a "deflating experience and helped lead to their collapse." Whether this was the reason for its collapse or not, he clearly had no idea back in the planning stages of the HKIA evacuation how quickly that would happen.

This isn't the book—and I'm not the writer—to try and explain the political history of our adventure in Afghanistan. Nor am I a political scientist or a professional war historian. If you were to ask me for a word to describe our involvement there, "clusterfuck" is the one that comes to mind first.

I would recommend anyone who's interested in learning more to read *The Afghanistan Papers* by *Washington Post* reporter, Craig Whitlock. Just as the Pentagon Papers revealed the political decisions that drove the Vietnam War and led to politicians and the Pentagon spoon feeding disinformation to the public, *The Afghanistan Papers* does the same.

The newspaper sued the U.S. government twice to gain access to the documents that form the basis of the book. It shows that the American public has been lied to by our government in a massive way for 20 years. It's so damning—and depressing—I'm tempted to use every colorful adjective I can think of to describe its findings. But all I'll add is that it's mind boggling to me that our highly educated policy makers and senior military leadership didn't bother to try and understand a country that ended up costing us so much blood and money.

As Whitlock wrote, "To an ignorant foreigner, Afghanistan's history, complex tribal dynamics, and ethnic and religious fault lines felt bewildering. It was much easier to divide the country into two camps: good guys and bad guys."[1]

Easier, sure, but 20 years later, while the cast of characters had changed, the problems on the ground remained the same.

Shortly after the majority of U.S. troops had withdrawn at the end of April, the Taliban flexed its muscle and began overrunning a dispirited ANA in Balkh, Takhar, Faryab and Kunduz Provinces up north, while the Pentagon began planning with the State Department

---

[1] *The Afghanistan Papers*, Simon & Schuster, New York, 2021, pages 20–21, Craig Whitlock.

for the evacuation of American civilians and Afghan allies before the August 31 deadline.

By the time that Marine Brigadier General Farrell Sullivan arrived at HKIA as commander of the Joint Task Force Crisis Response Team (JTF-CR) on July 20, the Taliban were on the move and were approaching larger population centers like Mazar-e Sharif, Kandahar, Kunduz, and their ultimate prize—Kabul.

Despite their obvious progress, U.S. intelligence officials were painting a much rosier picture. In a White House meeting on April 24, administration officials agreed on a plan to pull the 3,500 troops at Bagram Air Base by July 4 and leave 1,400 employees protected by a force of 650 Marines at the embassy to conduct business. The plan was reliant on U.S. intelligence agency estimates that the ANA could hold off the Taliban for another 18 months.[2]

On May 17, the CIA issued a report predicting that President Ghani's government would hold until at least the end of the year. The Defense Intelligence Agency was even more optimistic, predicting on June 4 that the Taliban would only be able to seize rural areas, and that Kabul would stay under government control indefinitely.

Many Afghans knew differently. Maybe it's because they inherently understood the geopolitics of their country and they recognized that, without the support of America, the ANA was a paper tiger. Many Afghan soldiers fought bravely over the years, and many died doing so, but the concept of a unified and effective national army in a country dominated by tribal politics had been conjured up by us—and we were leaving.

The interpreters who worked with American troops were especially good at reading the cards on the table. In June, a group of them protested outside the U.S. embassy in Kabul about the lack of Special Immigrant Visas (SIVs) being issued by the State Department. President Biden had made a promise in April that our Afghan allies would be granted expedited SIVs and relocated to America.

At the time, there was a backlog of 18,000 Afghan interpreters, drivers, security guards, clerks, fixers and 53,000 of their family members waiting

---

2   *New York Times*, 8/21/21.

on an SIV, a program that had been implemented by Congress in 2006. The waiting time averaged 3.5 years, according to No One Left Behind, an NGO working to get them out.

The protestors' sense of urgency about leaving the country was heightened by the fact that over 300 interpreters or family members had been ruthlessly hunted down and killed by the Taliban in the previous seven years. In 2014, Zaibullah Mujahid, the official Taliban spokesman, told VICE News, "They will be targeted and executed like foreign soldiers and foreign occupiers."[3]

According to No One Left Behind, 90 percent of an estimated 50,000 interpreters who worked with coalition troops in the country reported receiving death threats from the Taliban.

Neither the Pentagon nor the State Department kept a central database of how many Afghans were eligible for the program. The International Rescue Committee said in an August, 2021 report that 263,000 Afghans who remained in the country were eligible, but that number isn't confirmed anywhere else.[4]

It's not a surprise that no one knows the true number of eligible SIV applicants. A 2020 State Department internal audit of the SIV program cited "serious shortcomings" in the program, for reasons including staff shortages and the lack of a centralized database.[5]

One of the problems in documenting and determining eligibility for Afghan allies is that they weren't hired by the U.S. government, but instead by private contracting companies who bid on providing logistical support services to the Pentagon and State Department. These companies represented a seismic shift towards the privatization of America's war efforts since 2001.

Of the $14 trillion we spent on the wars in Iraq and Afghanistan since the turn of the century, an estimated $5 trillion has gone to private contractors.[6] Anyone who doesn't think war is big business needs to look at those numbers again.

---

3   Vice News website, www.vice.com, "The Interpreters," 8/14/14.
4   International Rescue Committee website, www.rescue.org, 8/2/21.
5   *New York Times*, 6/10/21.
6   *Profits of War: Corporate Beneficiaries of the Post-9/11 Pentagon Spending Surge*, www.watson.brown.edu, William D. Hartung, Center for International Policy, Brown University.

Many of them are household names: Lockheed Martin; Boeing; Northrop Grumman; General Dynamics, for example. But the LSPs (Language Service Providers) are mainly privately held companies that fly under the radar. Most sprang up overnight to fulfill the massive need for interpreters (spoken word) and translators (written word) in Iraq and Afghanistan.

Take Mission Essential, a Columbus, Ohio company started by two retired Army Special Forces veterans in 2004. By 2007, it had been awarded a $700 million contract by the Army Intelligence and Security Command (INSCOM), which is responsible for awarding LSP contracts, among other things.

The company cracked the $1 billion mark in Pentagon contracts by 2010. I can't think of any other industry—except narcotics—in which you can go from startup to $1 billion plus in six years.

Mission Essential's principal shareholders were reaping the rewards, but the same can't be said for its Afghan employees. In 2009, as it approached the $1 billion revenue mark, it was paying local interpreters $900 a month on average. They were expected to work 84 hours a week and be on call whenever needed. In less than three years, 24 of them were killed fulfilling their Mission Essential contracts.

Financial success, of course, breeds competition. Dozens of other LSPs have sprung up over the years. In 2017, INSCOM awarded a $9.86 billion linguistic services contract to nine separate companies, including Mission Essential.

Back to the problem as it relates to these private contractors and the Afghan SIV program. Over the years, dozens of these companies, whose employee base consists mainly of Afghan nationals, have been bought out, merged, or changed corporate identity.

When any of those things happen, records can get lost, scrubbed clean, or thrown in a paper shredder. At the time, it might appear to be a case of simple incompetence, laziness, or at worst, corporate malfeasance.

But when you're an Afghan who worked at great risk for one of these companies for years, and you now desperately need proof of employment to get an SIV and get out before the Taliban kills you or your family, it's a much, much bigger issue.

Take Dyncorp, one of the oldest and largest private defense services contractors in the country. In 2020, the year it was sold to Amentum, another giant contractor, it booked over $3 billion in government-related revenue.

As the military news website, *Task & Purpose,* documented in a 2021 report,[7] Amentum's responses to paperwork requests from its Afghan employees has been to create a maddening maze of bureaucratic red tape and automated voice recordings. Many have tried for months to even get a simple response to their requests for proof of employment to submit as part of an SIV application, a process that can be almost as maddening as the one Amentum has set up.

As a result, a number of former Dyncorp interpreters have been denied an SIV for reasons including "insufficient documentation," or "failure to establish faithful and valuable service." In the last three months of 2020, the State Department denied 1,646 SIV applications from Afghan nationals.[8]

Thousands of them did get out and relocated to America in the preceding years, but the SIV program was cut down by the Trump administration. In 2016, 3,626 Afghan interpreters received visas, in 2018 that number dropped to 1,649, and finally in 2020, only 1,799.

On May 6, 2021, a number of representatives from international refugee assistance groups working to get Afghan allies out of the country pleaded in a Zoom conference call with White House national security staff to waive the time-consuming SIV process and evacuate 100,000 Afghan allies as soon as possible.[9] Unlike U.S. intelligence officials, they recognized that the Taliban had spent its time preparing for the U.S. military departure, and the early reports from the northern provinces were a harbinger of things to come.

But their pleas fell on deaf ears, in part because it would have required an increase in U.S troops. Between April and July of 2021, over 5,600 SIVs were issued, a record amount for the program, but a drop in the bucket to meet the needs on the ground.

---

7   *Task & Purpose* website, www.taskandpurpose.com, 9/30/21.
8   *New York Times*, 6/10/21.
9   *New York Times*, 8/21/21.

While we're on the subject of the value of Afghan interpreters to American troops, consider how Marine Major Thomas Schueman describes his interpreter Zak, who was attached to his unit, 3rd Battalion, 5th Marines, in the volatile Helmand Province in 2010.

"It became quickly apparent that Zak was there to do much more than translate our words," he wrote in the book they co-authored, titled *Always Faithful*. "He was there to fight alongside us."

That should help explain to people why U.S. combat veterans feel such a strong connection and brotherhood with our Afghan allies. And it should help explain why there was such a strong negative reaction in the military community to our government's failure to live up to a promise we made to them.

During my involvement in *#DigitalDunkirk*, I can recall many bitterly angry comments from other participants about what was perceived as a betrayal of our Afghan partners, and in one case, a very well-known military community podcaster literally breaking down in tears as the topic was discussed.

Unlike some fighting forces (the Russians in Ukraine come to mind) we do not leave a brother behind. When I say brother, I'm referring to all Marines, soldiers, sailors, airmen, men and women. With women now integrated into combat units, they are our brothers as much as the men are. Two of the 13 Americans who died at Abbey Gate were female Marines.

It is the unwritten creed of every fighting unit in every branch of the U.S. military to not leave a brother on the battlefield. That's not always doable, but our service members have always demonstrated that they'll do everything humanly possible to bring wounded, killed or captured comrades home to American soil.

In our collective minds, our Afghan partners were our brothers. It didn't matter that we had very little in common—that we prayed to a different God, spoke different languages, ate different foods, and had different expectations for our future. What did matter was that these men and women put themselves in great harm's way to help us. And we expected our government to live up to our promise to get them out. I'm not naive enough to think that all Afghan partners did that for selfless reasons. In many parts of the country, the unemployment rate was high and the opportunities to earn a good income were very limited. Can you blame anyone who jumps on the chance to provide a much better life for their family?

And yet, they still had to accept the risk of having the insurgent groups who fought to kill Americans for 20 years, finding out. First Al-Qaeda, then the Taliban, with ISIS-K lurking in the background.

It wasn't just their own personal safety they had to worry about. It was their families' as well. Many of them came from small villages, where, like every small town anywhere on the globe, there are ethnic and religious fault lines, generational grudges, nosy neighbors, and loose tongues. If a hostile group was hunting for one Afghan who they suspected of working for the Americans, they might not find him or her, but they'd find their family. At the least, they'd be threatened to reveal their whereabouts.

I saw this play out later with a family I was trying to evacuate. The family has a son in the U.S. Air Force. When the Taliban came to their neighborhood, that secret was discovered, most likely due to a neighbor being threatened for information. This led to their home being shot up. I still have the pictures of the bullet holes in the interior walls of the house.

Luckily they escaped, but as of the time of writing, they are still stashed away in a safehouse in northern Afghanistan. Unfortunately, according to the current SIV program, they don't qualify for a visa. I'll say that again: the immediate family of a current U.S. Airman, who are being actively hunted by the Taliban, don't qualify for a visa.

Others that have been found in this situation have been kidnapped or killed. The Taliban have decades of experience in knowing how to terrorize a local population to get the information they want. They did it then and they're doing it now.

CHAPTER 7

Marines Make Their Way to HKIA

The Marines of the 2nd Battalion, 1st Marine Regiment, 1st Marine Division are a proud bunch, and for good reason. Known as "The Professionals," they serve in a unit that has distinguished itself since its formation in 1922 in the occupation of the Dominican Republic, and again when it was reactivated in 1942 to fight in the World War II Pacific campaign.

There, 2/1 Marines were in the middle of many epic battles, including Guadalcanal, Peleliu, and Okinawa. In 1950, they took part in the legendary Battle of Chosin Reservoir in the Korean War, where 30,000 UN troops fought off a Chinese force of 120,000 in temperatures that dropped as low as –35° F.

Later, in Vietnam, 2/1 Marines fought the Viet Cong in a series of clashes in Quang Tri Province from 1965–71, and in 1968 the battalion took part in the Battle of Hue City, one of the most bitterly contested battles of the war and the focus of the classic war movie, *Full Metal Jacket*.

More recently, 2/1 took part in the First Battle of Fallujah in Iraq in 2004 and engaged in combat operations in Karabilah and Husaybah. In Afghanistan, the battalion deployed to Helmand Province in 2011, where it cleared one of the last Taliban strongholds in the Garmsir District along the Helmand River.

With that decorated history and a name like "The Professionals" to live up to, today's 2/1 Marines are a highly motivated and trained unit—although I would say that about any Marine, because that's how they've always come across to me whenever I encountered one during my time in the Army.

"The Few, The Proud, The Marines": it's just a slogan, but it describes them to a tee. I'd like to think that every U.S. service member is proud of their unit. I know I was proud of my unit—486th Engineer Company, 983rd Engineer Battalion. It's just that Marines have the reputation of being a notch above. Let's face it, the Army has 485,000 active duty, the Marines only 180,000. The Marines are fewer, which makes them prouder. It makes perfect sense to me.

Until I made contact with Sergeant Zielinski, I hadn't given all this much thought, to be honest. But after the smoke had cleared from the HKIA evacuation and some of the adrenaline from being involved in #DigitalDunkirk had worn off, I found myself needing to write about the experience, which led to writing a rough manuscript—an info dump I think of as.

After rereading it, I had a thought: why not try to track down Sergeant Zielinski and talk to him? After all, there would be no story without him. Or at least, there would be no story I would tell. Because without him, there's a very good chance that Abdul, Mohammad, and their wives and kids would have been left behind with the thousands of other Afghans who were as desperate as they were to leave. They might have ended up watching the last C-130 lift into the air on August 30, their hopes for a good life for them and their kids destroyed. Instead, they're living a few miles away from me, doing whatever they feel like doing—listening to music, watching TV, getting an education, flying kites if they want to.

Zielinski told me his name during that impromptu phone conversation on August 25, 2021, but in the chaos and confusion, I didn't ask him to spell it out and I scribbled down a phonetic interpretation of the name I heard from thousands of miles away. It was V-A-L-E-N-S-K-I.

So to find him, I did what felt natural and went on Instagram. A military account I follow called Northern Provisions had made a post about HKIA that day so I figured that was the perfect platform to ask the question. I asked if anyone knew of a Marine with this name who was at Abbey Gate on August 25, 2021.

The responses came back instantly. One of the great things about communicating with people in the military is that you get responses to texts and messages almost immediately, for the simple fact that everyone understands that intel is only good if it's fresh.

One of the responses I got back was, "Do you mean Sergeant Zielinski of 2/1 Marines? He's a Weapons Squad leader. He was at Abbey."

As it turns out, that's exactly who I meant. A couple of messages later, I had his contact info. Shortly after that, I was on the phone with him. Again. Just a few days short of the first anniversary of the bombing.

This time, there was no yelling or gunshots in the background. He didn't have people yanking on his arms and legs, waving documents in his face. He didn't have to pivot to scan the area for an S-vest bomber as he spoke. He could take in a breath without feeling like he was going to vomit. The connection was fine. Both of us were a lot more rested than the first time we spoke.

Although we didn't know each other besides the brief conversation the year before, we bonded instantly, and talked for over an hour. Both of us shed a few tears as we shared memories. We were glad we found each other.

During one of our conversations, Zielinski told me that he knew four other 2/1 Marines who would want to talk about their experience. The memories these five shared later during Zoom calls gave me the most visceral understanding of what it was like to be at Abbey Gate the eight days that 2/1 spent there. I can honestly say I've never heard such gruesome, horrifying, depressing, heart-wrenching stories in my life, and I hope to God I never have to again.

At the same time, I can't recall ever feeling such an overpowering sense of respect for the courage and compassion that these young guys—all still in their early or mid twenties—demonstrated, both at Abbey Gate, and later on the Zoom calls as they described these images that are burned into their memories.

It makes me think of a quote in an article about Abbey Gate in which a senior Marine officer said something to the effect of, "My Marines are trained to be killers, but I was never more proud of them than when I saw them holding a baby, or comforting children and women."

By now, most people have probably seen the photo of Marine Sergeant Nicole Gee of the 24th MEU (Marine Expeditionary Unit) cradling a baby in her arms at the airport. She posted the photo on her Instagram account with the caption, "I love my job." A few days later, she was killed in the blast.

That could have been any of the 2/1 Marines at the gate, because the Afghans were so desperate and so fearful of the Taliban, they threw their children over barbed concertina wire, or pushed their child into the arms of a Marine and then turned and disappeared back into the crowd. It's the stories of these children that especially haunts them now.

Back in the planning stages for the evacuation, absolutely no one could have predicted that this would have happened. To my knowledge, no one drew up a nightmare worst-case scenario, but if they had, they would have probably drawn it up just like it unfolded.

In its 53-page summary report released in February 2022, USCENTCOM (U.S. Central Command, which is one of 11 unified combatant commands operating under DoD, the Department of Defense), said that planning for the NEO (noncombatant evacuation operation) began in April 2021.

The report notes that the organizational plan for the NEO called for joint planning between the Pentagon and the Department of State (DoS) and its embassy operations in Kabul. The massive embassy, built between 2006 and 2016 at a cost of nearly $800 million, had a staff of nearly 1,400 U.S. citizens and 2,500 Afghan nationals at the time.

The partnership didn't go well. In typically terse military jargon, USCENTCOM made it clear in its report how it felt about the State Department's contribution to the evacuation efforts. In an initial meeting between JTF-CR and embassy staff at HKIA on July 19 to discuss the imminent NEO, CENTCOM noted that they continued to plan for the operation, "but to little effect."

This was the first in a series of shots that Pentagon planners took at DoS officials for their perceived inability to recognize facts on the ground. This despite the fact that the State Department had issued an advisory on May 15 urging all U.S. citizens to make plans to leave the country.

By the next month, as the Taliban stormed the country and closed in on Kabul, DoS was in full blinders mode, according to CENTCOM.

"USFOR-A-FWD developed a trigger matrix for preparation and execution of the NEO and shared it with USEK (U.S. Embassy-Kabul) staff. USFOR-A-FWD used the trigger matrix as a tool to measure the Taliban's advancement and to convince USEK's staff to prepare for NEO. However, USEK's staff showed little interest in planning for NEO."

DoS has, of course, disputed the report's claims. Without taking sides in this finger-pointing exercise, the five 2/1 Marines and one Air Force rescue pilot who were interviewed for this book said that they never saw any State Department personnel at Abbey Gate to help screen Afghans for evacuation, and that they constantly received conflicting orders on what paperwork State required for eligibility. In their boots-on-the-ground assessment, the only contribution DoS made to the operation was to make a chaotic scene even more chaotic.

The initial plan was for evacuation flights to take off from both HKIA and Bagram, but the decision to turn Bagram over to ANA forces in early July prompted Pentagon planners to focus on HKIA. The Bagram decision was, and still is, a head-scratcher for most. When U.S. troops literally slipped away on the night of July 1 after shutting off the electricity at the airfield, it removed the most valuable U.S. asset from the drawing board.

Instead of having a heavily fortified and easily defensible facility with two operating runways and a huge infrastructure capable of mass evacuations just 25 miles from Kabul, the NEO planners were left with the one runway, limited infrastructure and the exposed and hard-to-defend position that HKIA presented.

From a tactical standpoint, it remains hard to understand. The Pentagon disputes the assertion that the ANA wasn't told of our decision to leave, which is said to have led to a crisis of confidence about their ability to hold on to Bagram. A spokesman for Afghanistan's vice-president claims the decision to abandon the airfield was the starting point of the Afghan collapse.[1]

---

1 ProPublica, www.propublica.org, Hell at Abbey Gate: Chaos, Confusion and Death in the Final Days of the War in Afghanistan, 4/2/22.

Whether that was the case or not, the end result is that the epicenter of American involvement in Afghanistan—the sprawling base that at one time housed tens of thousands of troops, a variety of fast food restaurants like Popeyes, Pizza Hut and Burger King, a shopping mall, gyms, video game rooms, even a Harley Davidson store—was in ANA hands for 45 days until the Taliban overran it.

Bagram also contained the Parwan Detention Facility inside a renovated hangar building. Built in 2009, the prison housed up to 3,000 Taliban, Al-Qaeda and ISIS prisoners. The U.S. handed control of Parwan over to the ANA in 2014 after a 2012 incident in which U.S. troops burned 46 Qurans which they claimed Taliban prisoners had used to pass messages to each other. Some Afghan base employees witnessed the burning, and when word got out, it spread like wildfire across the country. Five days of rioting by outraged Afghans led to 30 deaths, including those of four Americans.

That's not the only fallout from giving up control of Parwan. One of the Taliban's first orders of business when they seized Bagram and then Kabul from the ANA on August 15 was to release over 12,000 prisoners from Parwan and Pul-e-Charkhi prison outside the capital city.

Over 6,000 Taliban prisoners walked free, but inexplicably, so did 1,800 ISIS-K inmates.[2] ISIS-K was formed in 2016 by disaffected Pakistani Taliban fighters who felt that the Taliban wasn't devoted enough to jihad. The two groups are sworn enemies. After killing Omar Khorasani, the imprisoned ISIS-K leader in Afghanistan, they set the rest free to fight them another day. It goes to show that dysfunctional leadership is a universal condition.

One of those set free was Abdul Rehman Al-Loghri, the son of a merchant from Logar Province and a former engineering student at a school in New Delhi, India. He was arrested in a foiled suicide bomb plot in the Indian city in 2017 and transferred by the CIA to Bagram, where his interrogation led to U.S. drone strikes on ISIS members up to 2019.[3] It's a mystery how he survived in Parwan after he ratted on his ISIS colleagues and likely had them killed.

---

2 *New York Times*, 1/1/22.
3 *FirstPost*, India News, 9/19/21.

Twice lucky, Al-Loghri slipped into the chaotic streets of Kabul with other former Parwan inmates as the Taliban stormed into the city the same day. It was the perfect cover to navigate the road to redemption for the shamed jihadist.

Eleven days later, his path would intersect with 2/1 Marines at Abbey Gate.

★ ★ ★

As they left their home base of Camp Pendleton, California for a planned deployment to Kuwait and Jordan in March, 2/1 had no expectation of being sent to Afghanistan.

The first three or four months were fairly routine, Sergeant Zielinski recalls. They did exactly what they would do back at Camp Pendleton: train on a selected daily task and do it over and over until they could do it in their sleep. The only real difference was that their families were 8,000 miles away, and the searing desert heat was worse than California's Death Valley.

For Sergeant Kasey Williamson, 24, of Reno, Nevada, it was just another in a string of deployments that had taken him to Japan, Australia, South Korea and Peru since he enlisted in 2016. A squad leader alongside Zielinski in Weapons Company's 81mm mortar platoon, he recalled starting to hear rumors of a possible Afghanistan operation while the unit drilled in the scorching desert heat in Jordan and Kuwait, but he knew the rumor mill in military units runs 24/7, just as it always has. Until your gear's on the plane, you never know.

Like most of the Marines in Weapons Company, Williamson had never seen combat. The long-running Operation *Enduring Freedom* in Afghanistan ended in December 2014 and the follow-up Operation *Freedom's Sentinel* was a scaled-down counter-terrorism mission more suited to Special Operations forces.

But like most Marines, he was ready, even eager, for a fight. As the rumors increased in frequency, he imagined being engaged in a firefight with the Taliban. "I won't lie, it's every Marine's dream to go into combat," he points out.

Sergeant Jose Ramirez, 24, another Weapons Company 81 mm mortar squad leader, felt the same way. A soft-spoken San Marcos, California native who grew up just 15 miles from Camp Pendleton, Ramirez also enlisted in 2016.

Ramirez, Williamson and Zielinski were all close to one another, but Ramirez was especially tight with Zielinski, who he met at Infantry Training Battalion just after both had completed boot camp. "We were pretty much inseparable. Wherever he was, I was. He's my boy."

Lance Corporal Caden Bair was one of the junior members of Weapons Company 81s Platoon. A native of Omaha, Nebraska, he was 20 years old and had logged just 18 months in service when he packed up his gear for the Middle East deployment.

Corporal Corey Moore of Hoopston, Illinois was also just 20 when his 2/1 Golf Company deployed. Although a member of the same 2nd Battalion as the others, he belonged to a different company.

That distinction is like living in the same apartment versus living on the same apartment building floor. He and the other guys knew each other enough to say hi when they saw each other in the chow hall, but they weren't buddies.

In the Marines, like other services, friendships are forged through proximity and time, but it can often be the luck of the draw that determines who those friends might be. Moore had his own unbreakable bonds with his Golf Company colleagues.

A standard Marine battalion complement is 730 Marines on average. A company size is around 100–250. At the platoon level, it's 25–50. At the squad level it's around nine, and finally, at the fire team level, it's just three to four. The smaller the unit, the tighter the bond between its members. It's basic math and simple human behavior.

These standard numbers were drastically reduced for this Covid-19 era deployment though. Like other U.S. military branches, the Marines had a sizable number of its troops refuse to be vaccinated for one reason or another. By the time 2/1 was on its way to Kuwait, nearly 40 percent of the entire U.S. Marine Corps had declined vaccination, which made them ineligible for deployment to certain Middle East countries.[4]

---

4   CNN, 4/10/21.

That figure is consistent with the manpower shortage that Weapons and other companies in the battalion experienced for the deployment, Zielinski recalls.

Although it was DoD policy, the military couldn't force service members to be vaccinated then because the vaccines were only authorized for emergency use by the FDA. They could, and did, limit their eligibility for travel and overseas deployment though. Since a number of vaccines have received authorized FDA approval and the new DoD enforcement policy came into effect, over 1,000 Marines had been administratively discharged by early 2022 for refusing vaccination.[5]

It is not a memory Sergeant Zielinski likes dredging up. The decision by some of his fellow Marines to choose this hill to die on—to value personal autonomy or politics more than the sworn oath implicit in the meaning of *Semper Fi*—bothered him a lot then, and it caused tension at every level of the battalion, he says. On a logistical level, it also caused them to be short-handed at HKIA and Abbey Gate at a time when every able-bodied Marine was needed.

The ones who did deploy were busy training and starting to daydream about going home when they heard talk about a possible evacuation at HKIA. It caught their attention, but they were Marines and they had been listening to rumors since day one of their enlistment. So they put it on the back burner and kept their nose to the grindstone. They went to Jordan for two weeks, a welcome change of scenery from the barren and endless Kuwaiti desert. Zielinski and his squad leaders trained a unit of the Minnesota National Guard's mortarmen on the 81s.

Back at Pendleton, Sergeant Zielinski's wife, Gabrielle, was in late-term pregnancy with the couple's first child. Being separated for such a milestone event is almost impossible for civilians to understand, but it's all too familiar—and no less difficult—to military personnel and their spouses.

It became even more difficult in early July, when 2/1 got word that their deployment would be extended a month, possibly two. This fact made the rumor of an evacuation in Kabul more likely, so they started paying more attention to current events, especially those in Afghanistan.

---

5   U.S. Naval Institute website, www.usni.org, 3/10/22.

All the speculation became known fact on August 12. Zielinski recalls having his eyes glued to a TV screen when Pentagon spokesman, Admiral John Kirby, announced that 3,000 U.S. troops, including two infantry battalions of Marines currently in the Central Command area, were being sent to Kabul to help evacuate the U.S. embassy.

There was no longer any doubt about their next mission. 2/1 Marines, along with 24th MEU, the Army's 82nd Airborne, and a joint contingent of 1,000 Army/Air Force support personnel to facilitate SIV processing, were on their way to Kabul.

When Zielinski, Williamson, Ramirez, Bair and Moore heard the news they had similar reactions: they were excited; they were nervous; they were ready for anything.

"We had no idea what to expect," Ramirez recalls. "We just knew we were ready to go and do the job."

By the time their C-17 touched down at HKIA on August 17, the chaos in Kabul was in full swing and Abdul Rehman Al-Loghri was on the move, undoubtedly dodging the Taliban checkpoints that sprouted up around Kabul like invasive weeds in the two days since they had seized control of the city.

He had a job to do too.

CHAPTER 8

Underway With *#DigitalDunkirk*

July 12, 2021

On the afternoon of July 12, I sent a quick message to Abdul. As news about the Taliban's rapid advances through the Afghan countryside grew louder, I guess my subconscious prompted me to check in on him.

Me: "Hey brother, how have you been since the bases closed?"

One minute later, he responded.

Abdul: "Hello bor. (I had once misspelled "bro" in a text exchange with him, and I think he thought this was the correct spelling.) I fine how about you and your family they are good."

Me: "Yes we are good. Do you still have a job?"

Abdul: "We are on move one year ago we jobless."

Me: "How's life now that the Americans have left?"

Abdul: "It sir now tomach dinger. Can I call you bor?"

Me: "I will try to call you tomorrow. I'm at work."

Abdul: "It okey bor. You lucky you have job."

I managed to get ahold of him the next day via FaceTime and we spoke for an hour or so. His English had understandably slipped since leaving Camp Marmal, and there were a few "lost in translation" moments. I found out after a few chat message exchanges with him, his spoken English was easier to understand than his written version.

But I didn't need any translation to sense his anxiety over the news of the Taliban's march towards the capital. Even as our own intelligence analysts and diplomats were assuring people that their takeover was well over the horizon, Abdul, Mohammad and millions of other Afghans could read the handwriting on the wall.

He had already looked into the SIV program and linked me to a list of documents and recommendations he'd be required to produce to start the process. That included a recommendation from an American supervisor along with a threat assessment. It was the first time I saw the absurd amount of hurdles an applicant faces to complete the paperwork requirements.

To a native English speaker living in a high-speed internet world in a peaceful country, the prospect of gathering all these would be enough to make you want to give up before you start. Imagine what it would be like for an Afghan dodging bad guys in the midst of the total collapse of a lawless country.

Abdul asked me if I could fill it out for him. I told him I could not since I was not his supervisor. He was perplexed. In Afghanistan there are some rules, but they're more like guidelines. He didn't understand why I didn't have the authority to sign his recommendation letter.

I asked him if he had contact with his direct supervisor at Camp Marmal. He said he thought his name was Alex and said he worked at the mayor's cell. Most camps on foreign soil has a mayor and a mayor's cell, the purpose of which is to make sure every troop is safe, has a place to sleep and food to eat. The camp mayor is the man in charge of that effort. As an enlisted soldier, I never spent much time in the mayor's cell, which is where officers mingled and drank coffee while we worked.

With just the name Alex to go on, I called up the second lieutenant who I had served with in Afghanistan and asked if he remembered an Alex that worked at the mayor's cell at Camp Marmal. He searched through his emails from deployment and found one—Alex… I'm going to call him "Hernandez," since I speak ill of him and don't want to use his real last name.

I relayed the name over to Abdul to see if he recognized it.

"Yes, thanks bor." "Do you know him?" I told him I didn't but I had his email now and promised him I would reach out.

I emailed "Hernandez" the following:

Good afternoon sir,

    This is Sgt. Cook from the 486 EVCC, we worked with you guys at Camp Marmal in 2019–2020. Our LT was LT Barnette (CC'd on this email) This is a long shot, but a man named Abdul worked with us and recently reached out to me via Whatsapp asking for help. Because of his activity assisting Americans at Camp Marmal, he is in fear of the Taliban and is trying to apply for a US visa. He is filing the paperwork, but to fill the requirements he needs a recommendation from a superior. He told me you were his supervisor, but did not have your email address. LT Barnette gave your email to me. Just curious if he reported to you or if there is someone else he should be reaching out to.

    I can also relay info from you to him. He's a good man, so I'm trying to help. Any info would be appreciated.

Thank you.

Sgt. Mikael Cook

He didn't reply. Frustrated, I emailed him again. Then I got his reply. After a lengthy email spewing all the reasons he couldn't help, he made it very clear in one sentence: "I am going to seek guidance from DHS and have to say I feel this is way above my pay grade and my main concern is that I could be putting my career and clearance at stake by getting involved in these matters."

Reading that made me nauseous. Later, as I saw people in positions of much greater importance put their ranks and reputations on the line to do the right thing, it became even more apparent how gutless it was.

Weeks later I was listening to a *Zero Blog Thirty* podcast with their guest, Marine Major Chris Davis, who was one of the early architects of *#DigitalDunkirk*, and a man who would help me immensely throughout the operation. He said to the podcast host, Chaps, "If you're not willing to put your rank on the line, you shouldn't wear it."

At this point I thought we were stuck. I remember sitting around the kitchen island at my home in Michigan with my family, when Abdul called on FaceTime and showed us his young children. My mother had a fake smile pasted on as Abdul lifted up his infant daughter. She was sick thinking about this baby girl growing up under Taliban control. When we hung up, I told my family I didn't think there was a way to get them out. It seemed like it was over before it even began.

But what I didn't know was that there was already a loosely connected group of people building the beginnings of a network that would eventually connect together like mycelium connects trees under the forest floor. It was just as organic in its growth, and eventually, just as awe-inspiring in its strength and efficacy.

I had no idea that people like Major Davis and Marine Major Tom Schueman had been at work for months trying to get Major Schueman's former interpreter out, and along the way they had been tapping into their networks and creating new ones as they went along. They were, as Major Davis told me in a conversation later, "building the airplane in flight."

Major Schueman had been a platoon commander with 3/5 Marines in Helmand Province and led his unit in one of the fiercest battles of the entire Afghanistan campaign. His interpreter, Zak, had first submitted an application for an SIV in 2016. Like so many other Afghan interpreters, he had been unable to provide the complete paperwork required because the American contracting company he was hired by had dissolved, and he had no access to his HR documentation.

The major had pulled every string available, even getting Illinois Senator Durbin to mention his case at a Senate hearing and to confirm that Secretary of State Blinken was aware of it and involved in trying to get Zak authorization to enter the U.S. In any other country, having that high level of support would get you a free pass to do almost anything, but in the red-tape bureaucracy of the dysfunctional American immigration system, it wasn't worth the paper it was printed on.

When it comes to supporting allies and the veterans they served with, Schueman walks the walk. He is also the founder and CEO of Patrol Base Abbate, a veteran support community with 43+ chapters in the United States.

Named after Sergeant Matthew Abbate, a 3/5 Marine who was killed in combat in Helmand Province in 2010, PB Abbate also provides veterans with a 60-acre retreat camp in Montana. Schueman said he founded it after three Marines in his unit committed suicide post-combat, and he discovered there were few resources available that would allow them to connect with other veterans before they reached that crisis stage.

Despite encountering roadblocks after Senator Durbin's intervention, Major Schueman was undeterred. In March 2021, he reached out on

Instagram to Major Davis, who was, and still is, an active duty lawyer in the USMC Judge Advocate Division. In addition to being a hell of a Marine and a born leader, Major Schueman is also a great judge of character.

Major Davis was built to be involved at the ground level in an unscripted complex operation like #*DigitalDunkirk*. I got a strong sense of that when we worked together on Abdul and Mohammad's exfiltration, but it was only after meeting with him in a D.C. coffee shop late in 2022 that it became very clear to me that his personality and skill set aligned perfectly with the immense challenges on the ground.

In addition to being personally driven to excel at whatever he did—a common trait with Marines—he's the kind of guy who can step back and look at the big picture, and then design a solution to solve a specific problem. Now it's true that plenty of people can design solutions, but what makes him truly unique in my mind is that he's able to build and use the tools to implement that solution. Couple that with his never-quit motor and his sharp intelligence, and you have a pretty formidable force.

Originally an MP stationed in Okinawa, Major Davis deployed to Afghanistan in 2011 as security support for a special task force assigned to help the government of Afghanistan establish a rule of law and write a constitution. At Camp Phoenix, outside of Kabul, Davis witnessed officers in the Judge Advocate's Division hammering out constitutional details with members of the Afghan Shura. He basically had a front-row seat to a nation-building process. That experience ultimately led him to law school and a career as a Marine lawyer.

People like Majors Schueman, Davis and others were building chat forums, adding new people and delegating along the way. So too was former Green Beret, Scott Mann, who reached out to his Special Forces community in forming Task Force Pineapple, an organization that became heavily involved in exfiltration efforts from the very first days.

Others, like Tony Marcus, were raising money and building awareness. An Instagram meme creator who posted under the name Quentin Quarantino, Marcus started a GoFundMe campaign to raise money to pay for charter evacuation flights. Operation *Flyaway* eventually raised over $7 million.

Oblivious to all this, I checked in with Abdul on August 15. I still had little hope of a solution to getting them out, but I didn't want him to feel like I abandoned him.

It was an auspicious day to contact him, to say the least. It was the day that the deck of cards finally collapsed. President Ghani abandoned his people and fled to Uzbekistan and then on to the United Arab Emirates. The ANA responded predictably to the news and laid down their arms. Fight for what? Who? In a scene straight out of Saigon, 1975, the acting U.S. ambassador and embassy staff evacuated the embassy in a helicopter to HKIA and then boarded a flight out of the country.

Most ominous of all for Kabul's residents, the Taliban took over the city unimpeded. It took just 1,000 of them to take control of a city of 4.5 million people.[1] Just like they had done 25 years before, Abdul, Mohammad, and their families locked their doors, drew their curtains, and withdrew in despair.

"How's it going bro?" I wrote. It looks like such a silly and pointless question now, seeing it in print.

"Brother they get all Kabul. We are hiding. What about Alex did he answer you?"

I knew "Hernandez" wasn't going to write a recommendation, but I didn't want him to give up hope.

"No, I haven't heard back from him yet."

That's all I had for him at that point. I could sense his fear and frustration, but I felt helpless about helping them. The idea that I was his only lifeline to getting his family safely out of the country was almost overwhelming. I wasn't a high-ranking officer, or a senator's son, or a CIA covert ops guy with a little black book full of in-country contacts. I was a staff sergeant in the U.S. Army, 7,000 miles away in rural Michigan.

On August 16, I listened to President Biden play the blame game in his TV address to the nation by claiming that the collapse of the Afghan government was entirely the ANA's fault for giving up the fight. Frankly, it made my blood boil to hear him simplify and deflect by saying they "didn't have the will to fight." That would be news to the estimated

---

1 *New York Times*, 12/19/21.

69,000 Afghan security forces who died fighting as our allies between 2001 and 2021.

Another number that comes to mind is the five draft deferments President Biden received to avoid going to fight in Vietnam, which is only one more than the four deferments President Trump got. Who was it that didn't have the will to fight?

To burn off some steam and frustration, I hopped in my truck that night and drove into town to play hockey. On the way, I listened to *Zero Blog Thirty,* which is produced by Barstool Sports and hosted by three U.S. military veterans. They had the same reaction to Biden's speech as I did. One of the hosts, Kate Mannion, actually broke down and cried as they talked about the shame and anger they felt at what appeared to be our complete abandonment of our Afghan allies.

Kate summed up my feelings by saying, "America is better than this. We let these people down. It wasn't a war against Afghanistan, it was a war with Afghanistan against the Taliban. Tens of thousands gave their lives and worked side by side with us. It's such a slap in the face that we couldn't even keep our promise to those that put it all on the line for us."

I wept along with her as I drove down the road. It was the first time I had cried in a long time. All those people that helped us were being abandoned. Why would anyone ever want to help us again? We were planning to leave tens of thousands of people that had assisted us for the last 20 years. What does that say to our future allies? What it says is this: if you help us and are looking for safety in return, don't count on it.

On August 18, the day that Majors Schueman and Davis were finally able to get Zak and his family on a flight out of Kabul, I got word of a miracle as unexpected as a lightning bolt from a clear blue sky: Brian Wilhelm, a civilian contractor who served as camp mayor at Camp Marmal before I got there, heard on the grapevine that Abdul and Mohammad needed a letter of recommendation and was willing and eligible to write it.

> Abdul's outstanding service to the soldiers and contractors of Camp Marmal distinguishes him as a mature individual who is loyal to the USA. As a result of Abdul's work-based activities for the U.S. Government, I can verify that the risks are significant and genuinely do have an impact on his personal safety and

the safety of his family in Afghanistan. I believe that amid the deteriorating security situation in Afghanistan, Abdul and his family will be forced to flee the country. In view of this, I recommend Abdul for the SIV as he will make positive contributions and become a useful and productive immigrant.

We finally had some momentum!

I immediately began the process of applying for SIV visas for both men. I called and emailed state and federal officials, and was pleasantly surprised to hear back from Michigan's U.S. Senator Debbie Stabenow's office almost right away.

When I informed the senator's aide that we had two SIV applicants on the ground in Kabul and needed to start thinking about evacuation options, she asked that I send all the information I had on the two men and said she would do her best to push their case up the chain to get case numbers.

"Have them shelter at home until they're contacted," she suggested. I needed her help expediting the SIV and getting a case number, so I agreed. But even though I was a novice in the process, I knew enough about the pace of government action to know that having them sit around and wait was not going to be a good option.

When night fell on August 18, I had mixed feelings about what took place that day. Yes, we had the HR letter and had begun the SIV process. But I instinctively knew it wasn't enough to meet the deadline. Somehow, I would need to find another way, and I would need to do it fast.

In Kabul, 8.5 hours ahead of me in Michigan, the sun would soon come up on August 19. Sergeant Zielinski and the rest of Weapons Company, 2/1 Marines had landed at HKIA two days before.

Outside the airport, the crowds were growing rapidly and their anxiety along with them. The sharp staccato sound of the Taliban's AK-47s was so omnipresent by this time that one 2/1 Marine commented later that he got nervous when he *didn't* hear gunfire. In his mind, it meant something bad was about to happen.

2/1 Marines got their next order: proceed to Abbey Gate, which had just opened to process evacuees.

CHAPTER 9

Abbey Gate

"You Could Feel the Desperation to Your Core"

When the 2/1 Marines arrived at HKIA, the chaotic conditions that existed inside the airport on August 15 and 16 had improved. Like many horrified people around the world, they had seen the video images of Afghan civilians falling from taxiing Air Force C-17 Globemasters onto the tarmac.

That frenzied push by Afghan civilians onto the HKIA runways was stoked by news of President Ghani's departure and the evacuation of the U.S. embassy. Tens of thousands of people stormed into the airport.[1] According to the Central Command summary report, there were only an estimated 1,600 U.S. and coalition military personnel at the airport initially to stop them.

But they were able to piecemeal a large enough deterrent force to clear the airfield after a Herculean two-day effort. The arrival of elements of 82nd Airborne helped greatly. So too did a contingent of 1,200 Afghan National Strike Force (NSU) members.

Also known as "Zero" units, they were CIA-aligned soldiers who had a reputation for playing fast and loose outside the lines. The CENTCOM report notes that they offered to help clear the HKIA airfield in exchange for a promise of evacuation for them and their

---

1   Task and Purpose, 10/10/21.

families. By some estimates, over 7,000 of the evacuees ended up being "Zero" unit members and their families.[2]

The most unorthodox assistance to the beleaguered HKIA protection force came from the Taliban, who offered Rear Admiral Peter Vasely, the overall commander of U.S. Forces-Afghanistan, help in clearing the airfield. Maybe they thought it would buy them goodwill from the U.S. government and improve their reputation in the eyes of the world. Or maybe they simply wanted to limit the number of Afghans who were able to leave by pushing them back outside the gate. Whatever the case, with flight operations at a standstill and a number of incoming troops like 2/1 Marines en route or scheduled to be shortly, Vasely accepted.

Nothing will make an Afghan crowd disperse as quickly as a heavily armed Taliban force baring their teeth. Using batons and metal rods and firing their AK-47s into the air over the crowd, they made short work of the job. When the ramp dropped on the C-17 the afternoon of the 17th and they stepped out, Sergeant Zielinski and other Weapons Company guys were surprised at how calm it was at the airfield.

A former defensive end on his high school football team, Zielinski said he had the same feeling stepping off the ramp as he did stepping on the football field on game day. "On the plane, I had the same pre-game jitters. But once my feet hit the ground at HKIA, they disappeared."

Before they got off the plane, Sergeant Williamson recalls telling the guys in his squad that there was no contingency plan to get them out. "I wanted them to know how serious a mission it was. It would be a lie to say we weren't scared some. It's every Marine's dream to see action, but there's some fear mixed in with the excitement. So I had a serious 'proud Dad' moment when they just looked at me calmly and said, 'let's do this.'"

They dropped their gear in a gym along with Echo and Golf Company, and then went immediately to replace 1/8 Marines to provide security on the perimeter between the civilian and military sides of HKIA. There, they dug foxholes alongside Fox, Golf and Echo

---

2   The Intercept, www.theintercept.com, The CIA's Afghan Proxies, Accused of War Crimes, Will Get a Fresh Start in the U.S., 10/5/21.

Companies, along with elements of the Army's 82nd Airborne, and sat through a mostly uneventful night.

The quiet was short-lived. The next morning they were sent to the PAX terminal to clear a route for a busload of journalists scheduled to arrive. The terminal was set up as a secondary-screening area for evacuees who had been passed through the gates. Even there, they got a sense of the desperation of the civilians. They also had their first face-to-face encounters with Taliban soldiers.

Williamson saw two women and a boy leaning against the terminal building, when a Taliban soldier called them by name and pushed them inside. "I've never seen human beings look as terrified as they did."

He watched Taliban soldiers drag two men away, and recalls that he instinctively knew from their body language that they were taking them to a location out of sight to shoot them. The mission rules of engagement (ROE) prohibited him from intervening.

"I was standing face-to-face, about 10 feet from them. My eyes were glued on them the whole time. This was the enemy that wanted to kill us, and had killed so many of our Marine brothers over the years. It was very, very, difficult to restrain ourselves."

Civilians weren't the only ones who were terrified of the Taliban. Sergeant Ramirez remembered having a quiet conversation with an ANA soldier outside the terminal. When he asked the soldier where he was from, he responded, Kandahar, but it didn't matter, because he knew he'd never be able to go home again.

Ramirez also got a sneak preview of the absurd scenes he would witness for the next 10 days when he saw another ANA soldier pistol whip a man in the face. Bleeding profusely, the man kissed the soldier on the cheek in return. "Believe it or not, I saw crazy shit like this all the time," he recalls.

While they worked the civilian terminal area to help process the flow of evacuees who had been vetted through the airport checkpoints, the crowds were swelling in numbers outside the gates.

After clearing the airfield to accommodate the arrival of the remainder of 82nd Airborne, 24th MEU, the remainder of 1/8 Marines and 2/1 Marines, Rear Admiral Vasely and Major General

Christopher Donahue of the 82nd Airborne turned their attention to the HKIA gates.

24th MEU were assigned to man the North and East Gates. The unit had been informed of their planned involvement for the NEO in June and had been preparing at a base in Kuwait since July, including staging a number of rehearsals. Of all the U.S. troops at HKIA, they appeared to be the best trained specifically for the mission.

However, the gates they were assigned to ended up being less than adequate to handle potential threats and crowds. CENTCOM notes in its report that North Gate was vulnerable to VBIED (Vehicle-Borne Improvised Explosive Device) attacks due to its lack of standoffs and barriers and its proximity to civilian roads. It operated intermittently and was eventually closed on August 23 because of the VBIED threat.

East Gate consisted of a single gate, and was at risk of being breached by the growing swell of Afghan civilians desperate to get into HKIA. Even before the giant, agitated crowds outside the airport on the 25th and 26th, people were frequently crushed along a perimeter wall. It was also vulnerable to incoming mortar fire, the report notes. It too operated intermittently, and was permanently closed on the 24th.

The closure of North and East Gates left two gates. One of them, Glory Gate, didn't even exist on paper and was kept a secret from the Taliban. The reason for this subterfuge was that it was operated by the CIA, manned by an Afghan paramilitary group known as 02, and used only for high-priority assets, including those selected by the White House.

The gate was located on the north perimeter of the airport about two miles from Abbey Gate. It was made of Hesco barriers and blast walls and extended as a corridor from the perimeter fence to the road, across the street from a gas station used as a meeting point.

I became aware of this gate later on when we attempted a last-minute evacuation of the family of a soldier from my unit. They made it to the gas station, but after a series of miscues, we had to abort the attempt, which led eventually to a long, harrowing bus ride for the family to Mazar-e Sharif and an agonizing month-long wait in safe houses.

As you could expect from an operation that involved so much risk, chaos, and had such a high level of personal commitment, the

CIA and Special Ops guys thrived in that environment. It demanded improvisation, relationship-building skills, risk assessment, and big balls, and these guys could deliver on all those. This mission was right in their wheelhouse.

One of these guys was Air Force Major Jared Lefaivre. The 39-year old Bardstown, Kentucky native is a helicopter rescue pilot who arrived in Kabul in July. Normally assigned to locate and recover downed pilots, on paper Lefaivre seemed like an unlikely candidate to get involved in covert civilian exfiltration missions.

But nothing about the HKIA operation was typical, and neither is anything about Lefaivre. For one, he's one of the few guys who can say that he's served in the Marines, the Army and the Air Force, all as an aviator. His skill set as a Marine officer and Air Force rescue pilot aligned perfectly with the demands of the mission.

Two, because he arrived at HKIA a month before the NEO got going, he was already familiar with the infrastructure, the terrain and the assets available at the airport.

Finally, he was in the same platoon as Major Schueman at The Basic School in Quantico, Virginia, so when Schueman needed help in getting his interpreter Zak out, Lefaivre was able to grab two Air Force Special Operations Pararescue Specialists (PJs) and head to Abbey Gate. It was the day before the gate officially opened to process evacuations.

"It was a Hail Mary pass," he told me in a Zoom interview a year plus later. "I knew that Major Schueman needed some help and I had some spare time, so that's what I did."

As soon as he agreed to help, the Marine in him switched on, Lefaivre recalled. His parents are both Marine vets, and it runs in his bloodstream. The three-man team geared up, trekked down to a spot near the Abbey Gate entrance, and threw a ladder up to climb up to the concertina wire. When he got to the top, he looked down to see a Taliban soldier looking up at him. They both grabbed for their weapons, barrel down, but at the ready. Like Lefaivre, the Taliban soldier clearly knew that raising the barrel meant a close-quarters gunfight.

"For the longest time we just stared at each other and didn't blink. It was a stalemate," he explains. The Taliban soldier finally turned and walked back to the ANA armored vehicle they had commandeered.

As he was climbing in, he simulated shooting Lefaivre with his thumb and index finger.

Relying on the photo and code words that Schueman had provided to him, his team found Zak and his family up against a wall near the entrance to the Baron Hotel complex about 300 yards from Abbey Gate. From there, they were able to lead them to an access door that led to a courtyard outside the hotel, and eventually through Abbey Gate proper into HKIA. After months of effort by Schueman and others, Zak and his family were safe.

Major Lefaivre and his team would repeat that mission countless times over the next week, including the day of the Abbey Gate bombing, when he frantically tried, but failed, to get an Afghan family in as the gates were being prepared for closing.

He also worked with Major Chris Davis to exfiltrate Afghan interpreter "Lucky," who survived a number of combat encounters with the Taliban while attached to Marine units. Altogether, Lefaivre was individually credited with evacuating over 200 Afghan allies, while the Personnel Recovery Task Force he was attached to during the HKIA NEO is credited with evacuating 3,800. He was awarded the Bronze Star for his efforts.

As the sun came up on August 19, Abbey Gate became the focal point of the NEO mission. It's a name that will be seared in the memory of the 2/1 Marines and everyone else who was there for the rest of their lives.

The gate was located on the south side of the airport, just east of the main road that ran in a straight line for three miles from the Green Zone, where the U.S. embassy, the presidential palace and many other significant government buildings were situated, to the main entrance of the airport. The gate was also just several hundred meters from Camp Sullivan, where I had spent a short time while on deployment.

It actually consisted of two gates, an advantage to controlling crowds that East Gate didn't have. It was structured from north to south, with the 10-foot-high steel inner Abbey Gate at the north end opening to the actual airfield. There was a 240-yard corridor between the inner gate and the outer gate to the south. That stretch was referred to as the inner corridor. The corridor had originally been designed to serve as a sally port for searching and processing incoming vehicles.

About 100 yards south of the outer gate, an egress road led to a complex of buildings known as the Baron Hotel. This was where paratroopers from the UK's 2nd Parachute Brigade (2nd PARA) had set up a gate to screen and process British citizens and their Afghan allies.

Corporal Moore of 2/1 Marines Golf Company said his unit got a chance to train extensively with 2nd PARA in Jordan prior to being deployed to HKIA. He described them as excellent soldiers, and said the British and American troops were often shoulder to shoulder pushing back against the crowd during the time they were at Abbey. Sergeant Zielinksi said the Brits were a "great unit. Very professional and friendly."

When Abbey Gate opened on August 19, 2/1's Golf and Fox Companies, along with battalion snipers, were assigned to the outer gate. They joined 2nd PARA and some members of an Air Force Pararescue team in an effort to open the gate and begin processing applicants.

But, as the CENTCOM report makes clear, they were almost immediately overwhelmed by the size and desperation of the crowd, which pressed forward with a combined mass and ferocity that none of them expected. It became clear almost immediately that the Marines would need to reconfigure the gate, or there was a good chance the crowd would breach the airfield again.

For the Afghans, it was a classic Catch-22 situation. In their desperation to get into HKIA, they posed the threat of shutting down flight operations again. That would, of course, limit everyone's ability to get out. But given the fact that the Taliban were roaming free beating and sometimes shooting them, that logic went out the window.

After processing just 750 evacuees that day, Golf Company's commanding officer, Captain Geoff Ball, tapped his 1st Platoon to lead the way in pushing the crowd of thousands back 200 yards beyond the outer gate past the egress road to the Baron Hotel to establish a choke point and additional checkpoint.

Corporal Moore can never forget the sight that he saw when he hopped out of the back of a truck commandeered by 2/1 and then lined up to form a wedge with his fellow Marines by holding each other's tactical vest straps and pushing forward as one.

"The level of desperation of the Afghans was insane. We just looked out on a sea of desperate people, screaming, pushing papers in our faces. They were trampling on each other. The men, especially, were acting insane. Kids were getting trampled by them and they just kept pushing forward, shoving their documents at us."

In the day-long rugby scrum that followed, it took the Marines more than eight hours to move the crowd back. By the end of their first day at Abbey Gate, the Marines had already gotten a sense of the physical and emotional demands of the mission.

The effort was worth it though. 24th MEU engineers were able to move some heavy equipment down about 40 yards past the Baron Hotel egress and hoist six shipping containers into position to form what became known as the Chevron—named for its inverted V-shape pattern. That configuration eliminated VBIED threats, and also established a bottleneck to keep the crowds from gathering en masse.

Once the Chevron was established, the Taliban began screening Afghans outside the containers before passing them through to 2/1 Marines in the outer corridor between the Chevron and the outer gate. There, 2/1 had established a holding area for evacuees to search them and examine their documents, before moving them to the inner corridor between the two gates for a more thorough search. Finally, evacuees were passed through the inner gate into HKIA for a final screening with State Department personnel before they were approved for evacuation.

On paper, it seemed like the best quick-fix solution to a bad problem. The CENTCOM report noted that, "between August 20th and August 25th, gate operations took on a structured and predictable battle rhythm. Crowds were desperate but manageable, able to be kept calm at Abbey Gate because Marines interacted with the people continuously."

On the ground, though, it was a different story. Yes, the crowds were more "manageable," but as the days went on, their desperation increased. The "calm" that the report describes is a word that only a public affairs officer sitting in a climate-controlled room back at HQ would use to describe the conditions at Abbey Gate. For example, seven Afghan civilians were reported to have been crushed to death in the crowds on August 21 alone.[3]

"The smell was grotesque," Zielinski recalls. "There was an overwhelming aroma of death at the gates and it increased as time went on. People got trampled to death and their bodies lay where they fell until UK 2nd PARA could sweep the area, pick them up and stack them near the Baron Hotel egress road."

"I saw a kid of about five or six get trampled out in the crowd. I tried, but I couldn't get to him. There were just too many people. Grown men were stepping on him in an effort to get closer to us to show their documents. I saw the life leave his eyes," Sergeant Williamson recounts in a voice that leaves little doubt that the horror of that sight remains with him.

The desperation was unlike anything the Marines had ever witnessed. Some Afghan mothers were throwing their babies over the 12-foot T-walls (concrete barricades topped with concertina wire) blindly hoping there were Americans on the other side to catch them and take them to safety.

Some didn't clear the walls and got caught in the wire and bled out before they could be rescued by medics. It was a horrific sight that witnesses will never completely erase from their memories.

Sergeant Zielinski was standing near the Chevron with two 2nd PARA soldiers when a woman came to him and wordlessly placed a young boy of about four years old in his arms and then slipped back into the crowd and disappeared. He looked down to see that the boy was dead.

"I held that boy in my arms before I held my own son [who was born during the deployment]," he recalls. "I wanted to be mad at the woman for doing that, but I couldn't be. She had no chance to bury her son in those conditions. It was pretty fucking heartbreaking."

While the installation of the Chevron did play a major factor in crowd control, the involvement of the Taliban in acting as gatekeepers had a predictable result. Instead of filtering in through the shipping containers as intended, the crowd avoided it like the plague and started looking for alternative ways to access the Marines at the outer gate.

---

3   CNN website, www.cnn.com, 8/23/21.

Every 2/1 Marine I spoke to was unanimous in their opinion about the Taliban soldiers they encountered at HKIA. To sum it up in one word: evil.

Of all the hardships and frustrations they endured, the one that produces the rawest reaction is their memory of how they could only stand and watch as the Taliban brutalized Afghan civilians.

"In my opinion, the Taliban are evil, evil people," Zielinski says. "No matter how much they try to convey to the rest of the world they're not, we saw nothing but evil from them. Beating and killing innocent people. Using kids as pawns. They're absolute evil."

As hard as it was for him and other Marines, it was worse for the few combat-tested members of the battalion, he points out.

"They said that this mission [Abbey Gate] was way worse than any combat mission, because we couldn't retaliate for what they did to civilians or we might go to jail. It took a huge emotional toll on everyone."

The threat of a court martial and jail time was definitely effective, because Marines had every opportunity in the world to settle some scores for the Afghan civilians they saw getting brutalized.

Corporal Moore said a Taliban soldier leveled his AK-47 at a Marine in another Golf Company squad. In return, he said, a number of squad members trained their weapons on him, which led to a standoff before the Taliban soldier wisely lowered his weapon. It could have ended up much differently with less professional soldiers. That episode helps explain why 2/1 Marines are called "The Professionals."

After days of witnessing beatings, abductions and reported killings by the Taliban at the Chevron, Afghan civilians found a way to bypass them by circling around the checkpoint and climbing through a hole in a chain-link fence to access a sewage canal that ran parallel to the gate corridors.

The canal originally served as a natural barrier for the Marines on the east side of the perimeter wall and fence. It contained roughly 2 feet of fetid sewage runoff, which in usual circumstances is a deterrent for most human beings. Lance Corporal Bair spent the last two days of the deployment on the wall above it.

"The smell was unbearable," he remembers. "It sticks with me to this day."

But as the crowd began to bypass the Taliban checkpoint and enter the canal area, that deterrent no longer mattered. It began to fill up with Afghans waving documents at the Marines who stood on the 6-foot-high wall above them. Soon, it was so crowded, there wasn't a crack of light between them. By the 26th, Pentagon officials estimated 10,000 people were packed into the canal.

As bad as it was witnessing the behavior of the Taliban, 2/1 Marines say it was equally as hard having to decide who would be allowed in the gate. It was, they all say, an agonizing responsibility for young Marines trained to fight, not screen visa applicants in the midst of chaos.

"Nothing could prepare you for the emotion at the gate," Ramirez says. "When I got overwhelmed by it, I tried to empathize and put myself in their shoes. They were hungry and thirsty and desperate. You could feel that desperation to your core."

It didn't help, he says, that they received constantly changing instructions on what documents to accept. They supposedly came from State Department officials, he said, but he never saw one of them at the gate the whole deployment.

"First the yellow embassy cards were good, then they weren't, then they were again. I had sent a bunch of people with those cards away. I can't describe the guilt I felt over that."

Ramirez's buddy, Zielinski, has a vivid description of what that experience was like.

"It was like having to play God. Who got picked, who didn't? You had people's lives and their futures in your hands." He choked up as he finished that thought and struggled to compose himself.

"I couldn't imagine being an Afghan in that crowd and watching that. I just want to let them know that we tried as hard as we could to help them. Our guys would go back for a break and they would break down because they were so upset by what they were seeing. Then they'd put their helmets back on and get back to work."

Their empathy didn't extend to every Afghan civilian they saw, however. The Marines say they knew there were cultural differences between Americans and Afghans, but the behavior of many Afghan men at the gate shocked and angered them.

"They had a complete disregard for anyone but themselves," Williamson recalls. "I saw a man throw a kid into the canal to make room for himself on the wall. They used kids like carpets to get over the concertina wire. They acted like animals."

Moore said he was so incensed after watching adult men swipe bottles of water that the Marines had passed out to children right out of their hands, that he tackled one man and took the water away from him.

"I hate to say it, but a lot of the Afghan men acted like scum," Ramirez adds. "They would leave their own families behind just so they could get through."

In the sea of humanity all around them—estimates of 20,000 or more around HKIA from August 20 on—it was the faces of the kids that they remember the most.

Ramirez said it was the face of a girl of around 13 that has stayed with him. "She didn't have any documentation, so I had to reject her. She was crying and crying. I felt like I was rejecting my own sister who's that age. She's the first face I see in my dreams."

Zielinski too is haunted by the memory of a young girl. She approached him with another girl and a man, and ended up hanging on to his legs crying, "Please let my family live." But they had no documentation, so he had to bring them over to the British-run checkpoint where they would be released back into Kabul. The girl had incredibly bright green eyes, he recalls.

"I told them over and over, 'I'm so sorry,' as I brought them out. I still have trouble sleeping. I see her eyes."

There were some success stories, and they tried to cling to those. "I tried to have a 'win' every time we went out," Bair explains. "Getting a family through was a win, so I tried to remember that when I witnessed all that other shit."

Ramirez said a young girl speaking very good English asked him for help. When he questioned why her English was so good, she handed him her father's Virginia driver's license and explained that they lived there, but had come back to Kabul for a wedding. She helped him translate until he was able to round up her family of 10 and escort them into the airport.

This was the "structured and predictable battle rhythm" the CENTCOM report described during that time period. But to be fair, despite the shit show of coordination and the chaos that ensued, the number of evacuees getting through the gates and number of flights going out increased.

On August 23, the State Department announced that the U.S. military flew out 10,400 people in the 24-hour period, while coalition members evacuated an additional 5,900. That number set a record for the most evacuees in a 24-hour period, despite frequent shutdowns of the gates to relieve the pressure inside HKIA.

Back home in Michigan, I was hoping to add 10 more to that total.

CHAPTER 10

Team Wins—Getting Them Out

After cooling my heels for four days waiting for some kind of bureaucratic breakthrough on Abdul and Mohammad's SIV application, I knew we couldn't wait any longer. So, on the morning of August 23 I started messaging everyone on Instagram I could think of who had political or military connections that might be able to help.

As I speed-scrolled, I spotted an Instagram page for a news organization called Atlas News. They had posted a viral video of the crowds of Afghans hanging on to a giant Air Force C-17 Globemaster plane as it taxied down the HKIA runway. It was a gut-wrenching video to watch: hundreds of people running alongside the plane, grabbing the wheel wells, bodies falling from the sky as the plane retracted its landing gear. The fallen bodies still smoldered by the time U.S. troops got to them, having skidded across the tarmac.

I couldn't help but draw a parallel to the images from 9/11 and the people jumping from the burning World Trade Center towers. The war was ending the same way it started, bodies hitting pavement. Later, I read that among the Afghan civilians that fell from the plane that day at HKIA was Zaki Anwari, a 17-year-old rising star on Afghanistan's national soccer team. He couldn't bear the idea of never playing soccer again under Taliban rule, his brother said.[1]

Atlas News was posting real-time updates on what was happening at the airport, so I sent a DM to its Instagram account asking if they

---

[1] Associated Press, www.apnews.com, After Afghans Fell From Plane, Families Live With Horror, 9/21/21.

had any contacts that could help get Abdul and Mohammad and their families in. Surprisingly, I got an immediate response back with a list of contacts that might be able to help. It was the first of many times over the course of the next few weeks that I witnessed how motivated this random collection of strangers were to get as many Afghan allies out of the country as they could.

As I continued messaging the Atlas contact, he informed me that a Marine at HKIA had told him that there was an active IED (Improvised explosive device) threat at Abbey Gate, and for the time being they were only letting American passport holders through. It was also the first of many times I heard an IED threat communicated in a chat forum.

With the contacts they provided, Atlas News was instrumental in introducing me to the *#DigitalDunkirk* universe. Unfortunately, another news organization I won't name was also instrumental in introducing me to the whole world, because for some reason they put *my* contact information in a news story and said I was someone who could help.

Whether this was an honest mistake or irresponsible journalism, I've never discovered, but within minutes my phone and email were blowing up with messages from Afghans begging for help. Many were heartbreaking to read. Later on, I found out that the Taliban tracked these sources, because I would get calls from them screaming in Pashto at me, with the only identifiable English word being "motherfucker." I was more entertained than intimidated. I'm glad they know I exist.

My next move was to reach out to Chaps, Kate, and Cons, the three hosts from Barstool Sports' *Zero Blog Thirty* podcast. I asked them all the same question: "Do you have any contacts at HKIA who could help me get my guys in?" As inundated as they were with messages, all three got back to me within a few hours.

Chaps referred me to Major Chris Davis' Instagram page. As I explained earlier, he became an invaluable resource down the road. But it was Kate Mannion who really stepped up and provided me with the encouragement and support that kept me going throughout the process.

Kate's a former Marine who did two tours in Afghanistan. She's also a former intern at Comedy Central and one of the funniest, most irreverent, and authentic people I've ever heard.

Here's our initial text exchange:

> Me: Kate, do you have any contacts at the HKIA gates? I have two SIV applicants making a run for the airport tonight. Looking for some intel on the ground.
> Kate: Hold on, let me check. Confirmed SIV? Let me know because I have a contact there but they need to know for sure if SIV.
> Me: No. They're still awaiting approval which has been taking forever. Senator Stabenow is trying to push their case through but no word from her yet.

I then sent her the applications to pass along to her contacts.

> Kate: So infuriating their life is on the line because of paperwork red tape. Fuck. Checking with the contact now and sending this info along.

She then put me in touch with a lieutenant in CENTCOM who was in charge of getting people registered on an evacuation list to extract people from the crowd at HKIA gates. I knew getting them on this list would greatly increase their chance of entry if we could lead them to the front. I thanked Kate for her help.

> Kate: We're just passing stuff along and linking people up. You guys are the great ones not leaving people behind. It's amazing to see. I'm so sorry you guys are the ones having to step up and do it.

I didn't feel then and I don't feel now that I deserve any credit for the effort. But that exchange with Kate—and many others to follow—motivated me more than ever to get my friends and their families out.

At 2:00 p.m. that day I took a break from messaging to call Abdul and advise him to get everyone together and make a run for the airport. He was staying in a home in Shahrak Arya, a new development neighborhood not far from the airport. In terms of a location for accessing the airport, it was ideal.

They scrambled to leave almost immediately. It was the two men, their wives, five young kids, and Abdul's younger brother, Massoud. It was midnight when they slipped out under the cover of darkness and wound their way through the side streets towards HKIA.

Abdul has told me he'll never forget the fear in their group as they made their way to the airport. One kid crying, one wrong turn into a Taliban patrol, and they would have been divided up for interrogation, or worse. It was eight days after the takeover of the city, and the Taliban were still unpredictable. Some soldiers were disciplined and practiced the restraint urged by their leadership (until the eyes of the international media shifted away), but many others were new recruits from small rural villages who were in a big city for the first time. Any encounter with a Taliban soldier was like rolling dice.

But, they made it unimpeded. Even though they were only a couple of miles from the airport, it took them several hours to navigate their way there. The crowds grew larger as they got closer. Abdul messaged me near the Abbey Gate entrance, including some photos of the crowd. It was so mobbed they had to leave their wives and kids further back to avoid having them get crushed.

He also began sending me voice texts. I could hear the screaming and chaos and desperation from thousands of miles away. It was obvious there was no control or order. At that moment, I knew this was going to be more intense and more difficult than I had ever imagined.

They were going to have to force their way to the front, and I would need to provide them with any information I could get my hands on to help them. But I soon discovered that another major hurdle was in communicating with Abdul near the airport. The mass population gathered in one spot was overloading the cell towers, the Taliban were jamming signals, and later I found out, so was the U.S. military in an attempt to disrupt any remote-controlled IED detonation.

So, every time Abdul wanted to call me on WhatsApp, he had to retreat back a good distance, losing any progress they had made in getting towards the front. Plus, each time they went back into the line they had to pass a Taliban checkpoint.

Mohammad got a taste of what could happen when that occurred. For no reason that he could identify, a group of Taliban soldiers grabbed him and beat him with an iron pipe around his neck and shoulders, as well as jabbing him in the ribs with the barrels of their AK-47s. He was quick enough and lucky enough to be able to slip away and disappear into the dense crowd.

It was obviously very dangerous for them to carry proof of U.S. government connections. Yet without documentation, they didn't stand a chance of getting out. For Mohammad, Abdul, and the tens of thousands of other SIV-eligible Afghans who showed up at HKIA, it was like carrying a lit stick of dynamite. While the sheer number of people helped create a human shield from the Taliban, the ones they did catch with U.S. government paperwork were badly beaten, or dragged away to meet a worse fate.

After struggling for hours to get through to the Chevron checkpoint, Abdul and Mohammad noticed a current of people diverting away from the checkpoint along the perimeter fence. They decided to join in, and eventually found themselves climbing through a chain link fence and jumping down into the sewage canal.

They pushed through knee-deep sewage water for 100 yards or so until they could go no further. From their vantage point, they looked up into the harsh white glare of spotlights that lit the area up like high noon in the middle of the desert. When their eyes adjusted, they saw a line of Marines and British paratroopers standing on the wall above them, no more than 15 feet away.

Abdul sent me a photo showing the crowd around him and the Marines above him. In the frame, I also saw the sniper tower where three Marines on duty scoped the crowd 24/7 for possible threats. It was almost the exact spot three days later where the ISIS-K bomber would detonate his suicide vest.

I asked Abdul if he could get close enough to hand the phone up to one of the Marines. "No brother, it is not possible, it is too much rush. The American soldier neither talks on the phone nor looks at the documents."

After 12 hours of pushing through to the canal and trying frantically to get the attention of the Marines, Abdul sent a voicemail recorded in an utterly exhausted voice. "May I take this opportunity to go to my house and hug my children?"

I felt a lump in my throat forming as I listened to it. All I could think about is how abandoned they must be feeling.

"Yes. Go get some rest and I will keep trying."

"That's right my kind brother, I'm waiting," Abdul replied.

I could tell from Abdul's voice message after this first attempt that he was confused. I was a non-commissioned officer in the United States Army, and he was standing 15 feet away from U.S military personnel, and I couldn't get him in. He didn't say it, but I knew he was thinking it. I had never been so scared to fail someone in my life. There was disappointment all around.

But I didn't have time to dwell on it. As sleep-deprived and depressed as I felt, I knew that if they were going to get out, I had to make deeper connections than the ones I made with Atlas News. I needed to give Abdul and Mohammad and their families a fighting chance to get out. That required more than a few well-meaning vets sitting at home like me texting one person they knew at the airport. While every small piece was helpful, it wasn't enough in the short time left.

So, I reached back out to Kate at Barstool, I figured with her notoriety, people would be hitting her up all day with intel and updates. I messaged her at 10:08 a.m. on the morning of the 24th.

"Just throwing you a quick update. Your guy got us on the USFOR-A-FWD evacuation list, so thank you very much. Still having trouble getting through the gate. If you have any other leads please let me know and thanks again."

"Do you have Signal app?" she asked. This was the preferred comms platform for the U.S. military. It was fairly secure, and yes, I did have it.

Kate then put me in contact with a woman named Haley on Signal. "If that doesn't work try Nick Palmisciano on Signal," Kate added.

Palmisciano is a legend in the military community. A former Army Ranger infantry officer, he's the CEO of the marketing company Diesel Jack Media, and Ranger Up, a military lifestyle brand that's sold over $100 million worth of tee shirts since its founding.

But what I didn't know then was that Nick and a few other special operators had just started a group called Save Our Allies. It ended up being the most effective organization devoted to evacuating our Afghan allies. They're the best of the best. If I ever get a chance to shake their hands, I'd be honored to do so.

Palmisciano, Special Forces legend, MMA fighter, and Ranger Up co-founder Tim Kennedy, Chad Robichaux and a team of nine others flew to Kabul, managed to convince the Crown Prince of the United Arab Emirates to lend them some planes, and over the course of 10 days are credited with helping over 12,000 Afghans get out of the

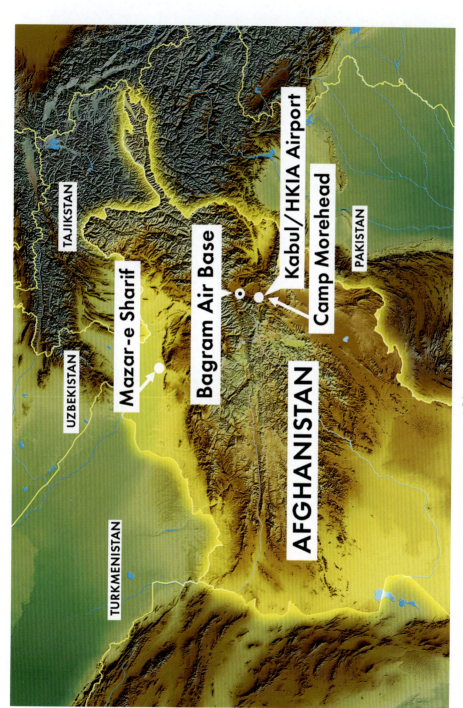

Afghanistan, 2021.

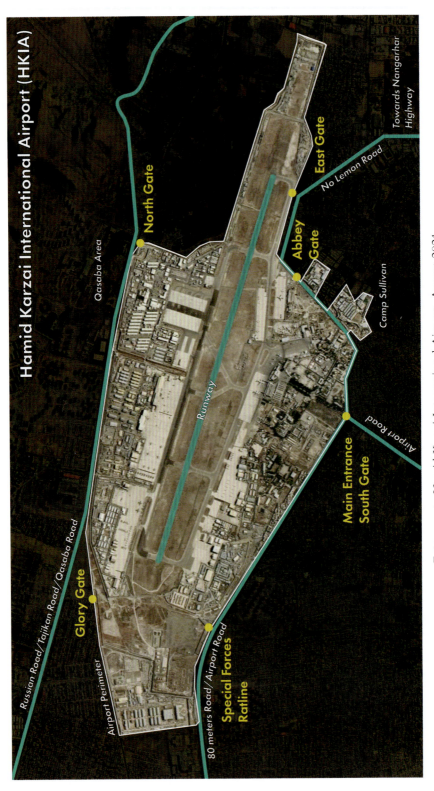

Entrances to Hamid Karzai International Airport, August 2021.

Mikael on patrol at Camp Morehead with Sergeant First Class David Zeleny and Sergeant Garrett Viars. (Author's photo)

Mikael saying goodbye to Mohammad and Abdul before leaving for Camp Morehead. (Author's photo)

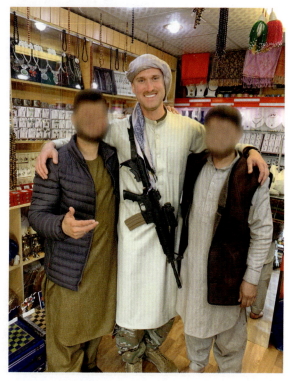

2/1 Weapons Company en route to HKIA on the C17. (Photo Sergeant Kasey Williamson)

The CIA-provided route, leading Abdul and Mohammad past Taliban checkpoints.

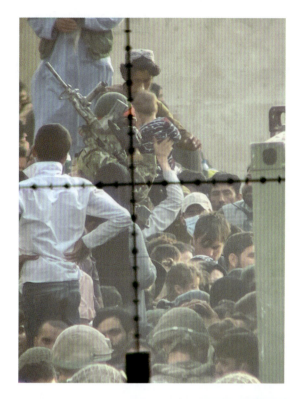

Marines monitor a Taliban fighter from the sniper tower at Abbey Gate. (Photo Sergeant Dalton Hannigan 2/1 Marines)

1/8 Marines manning the gate at East Gate. (Photo Corporal Ansel Rubin)

Screenshot of Mikael's text thread with Abdul at Abbey Gate. (Author's photo)

A U.S. Marine assists an Afghan over the wall at Abbey Gate. (U.S. Marine Corps photo by Staff Sergeant Victor Mancilla)

A Taliban checkpoint through the lens of a Scout Sniper Observation Telescope on August 20. (Photo Captain Bobby Barnhisel 2/1 Marines)

Abbey Gate vantage point from the sniper tower. (Photo Sergeant Dalton Hannigan 2/1 Marines)

1/8 Marines at North Gate on August 19. (Photo Corporal Mike Markland 1/8 Marines)

NCOs of 2/1 Weapons Company the morning of August 26, just prior to their shift at Abbey Gate. (Photo Sergeant Kasey Williamson)

Sgt. Zielinski sharing an MRE with an Afghan he helped evacuate. (Photo Sergeant Ethan Zielinski)

Marines sit atop a cache of captured weapons at HKIA. (Photo Corporal Mike Markland)

Afghans lining up to board an aircraft. (Photo Senior Airman Taylor Crul)

Sergeant Nicole Gee, U.S. Marine Corps. (Photo Sergeant Isaiah Campbell)

Group photo taken of the Paimans for the extraction team to identify the family. (Photo Paiman family)

Over 600 Afghans packed onto a US Airforce C-17 aircraft. (Photo Captain Chris Herbert U.S. Air Force)

Afghans loading a C-17 airplane to maximum capacity. (Photo Senior Airman Taylor Crul)

Major General Chris Donahue, Commander of the U.S. Army 82nd Airborne Division boards a C-17 as the last American service member in Afghanistan. (U.S. Army photo by Master Sergeant Alex Burnett)

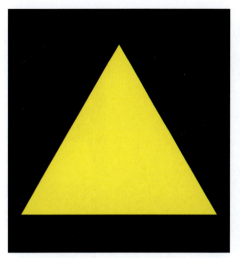

The "Challenge and Password" for the Paiman family to pass through the Special Forces Ratline.

Tracking the Paimans' Sayara flight until clearing Afghanistan airspace. It was the only plane in the air in the entire country.

Mikael at the award ceremony with the Paiman family, Avani, Captain Minnich and Senator Blumenthal's team. (Photo Army Specialist Coronado)

Mikael meeting with Senator Richard Blumenthal following the evacuation to discuss the current status of the Special Immigrant Visa program. (Photo provided by Senator Blumenthal's Communications Director Maria McElwain)

Mikael with Major Tom Schueman at a Patrol Base Abbate fundraiser in New York City. (Author's photo)

Mikael with Chaps from ZeroBlog30 at a Patrol Base Abbate fundraiser in New York City. (Author's photo)

Mikael with National Resistance Front Commander Massoud in Vienna, Austria. (Author's photo)

All of the children from the families Mikael helped rescue. (Author's photo)

Remains of the 13 KIA warriors killed in the blast at Abbey Gate. (U.S. Central Command Public Affairs Photo)

country. It was an amazing accomplishment. Most of us would have done anything to get on a plane to HKIA to help. They not only went to Kabul, they brought the evacuation airplanes with them!

I didn't know it then, but this was the point that I truly passed through the portal and entered the underground world of *#DigitalDunkirk*. I reached out to Haley and introduced myself and my situation.

> Hey Haley, this is SGT Cook. I have 2 Afghan SIVs that are also listed on the USFOR-A-FWD. They are having trouble getting through the gate. Is there any assistance available? I got your contact from ZeroBlog.

She replied right away: "I'm going to add you to a NEO comms group, hold on." She also asked me to not add anyone to the group without running it through Gabe, the guy running the group thread and facilitating operations.

I monitored the chat for a while to see what I had just entered. As I did, I felt a surge of adrenaline run through my exhausted body. It was amazing to see! This organic effort had developed real form and structure. In that one group alone, I saw over 50 people from different backgrounds—from combat vets, to active duty personnel to CIA case workers and operatives—exchanging real-time information and working on a long list of names that would end up being referred to as the "Digital Schindler's List."

The team had real-time information about which country was working which HKIA gate, who they were letting in and what documentation they required, as well as sharing contacts on the ground at the airport. As I watched this on my phone screen, the proverb "The strength of the wolf is the pack, the strength of the pack is the wolf," kept coming to mind. I became more confident now I had access to the right resources to get my guys and their families out.

As the chat lit up with conversation, I closely monitored it to determine who I thought could help me best. I began initiating sidebar conversations throughout the day if a relevant piece of information came across the chat. Over the course of the day, there were plenty of people who attempted to help me get through to their contacts at the gates. Despite these attempts though, in the chaos that was HKIA, I wasn't able to make any real progress.

Then came a sobering message over the NEO comms channel: "Taliban just put out that Afghans have 12 hours to leave Afghanistan before they close all gates from the outside."

My heart dropped faster than an elevator with a severed cable. I jumped right on the computer to fact check it. Like many things in this chat, it hadn't made it to the news cycle yet. But sure enough, 30 minutes later, it was a headline in several major news outlets.

Apparently upset about all the educated people—for example, the doctors, scientists, and engineers they'd need to keep the country from going back to the Stone Age—who were trying to flee, the Taliban said Afghans at HKIA should go home. Oh, and they said they wouldn't face any reprisals for trying to leave.[2]

This announcement came a day after CIA director, William Burns, met with Taliban leader Mullah Abdul Ghani Baradar, in Kabul to discuss the groundwork for the completion of the evacuation by August 31.[3] The White House and members of the G-7 dismissed the Taliban's announcement as posturing, and insisted that all eligible Afghan allies would still be allowed to leave the country by the original deadline.

In real time though, it was bombshell news. We didn't have the luxury of trying to figure out the nuances of the announcement. So, I called Abdul immediately. He had just gotten home two hours before after another long and dangerous journey with his family.

"Brother, I know you're tired but you have to go back right now, we only have 12 hours to get out."

He sensed the urgency through the phone.

"OK brother, I talk to Mohammad and we make our way to airport, I hope they check the list today."

"It's worth trying," I responded.

I couldn't even imagine how exhausted and anxious their kids and wives must have been and how reluctant they must have been to go back to HKIA. I'm sure both guys did their best to minimize the danger to keep them calm, but I do know that kids have an antenna for danger, so there's no way they wouldn't have picked up on it.

---

2   CNN, 8/24/21.
3   *Washington Post*, 8/24/21.

While they got everyone organized to go back out, I exchanged messages with a CIA officer who identified herself as only "JC." This contact was a game-changer, as JC provided up-to-date maps of Taliban checkpoints, as well as vetted routes to Abbey Gate where there would be a low risk of running into one of their soldiers. JC quickly escorted me into another sidebar with a few additional people looking for resources at Abbey Gate. By this time my phone was so hot from the constant barrage of messages coming in it could have scorched my hand.

I forwarded the CIA-provided map to Abdul. It was an aerial shot of the southeast sector of the airport with a blue line that snaked through side streets from a girls' secondary school to Abbey Gate.

He and Mohammad and their families headed right back out. Once they left the house, they went silent. My nerves felt as frayed as an old rope as I waited to hear from them. I couldn't escape the fear that I might be sending them to their death. Then I would think to myself, well if they stay, they might die too. It made it slightly easier to accept the risk.

"Break, Break, Break," someone on the NEO chat messaged. "Little boy stabbed at Abbey Gate."

Seeing that made my stomach churn. Why would anyone stab a little boy? The group had direct communications with a medical team on the ground, so it was likely accurate. The constant messaging of medical emergencies that came through the chat was sickening.

While Abdul, Mohammad and their families were still on their way to the airport, I reached out to the contact number Kate had given me for Nick Palmisciano. At the time, I had no clue how influential he was. I definitely had no idea that he had a full-size commercial jet at his disposal.

"Hey Nick, got your contact from Kate @ Barstool. I have 2 SIV that are at Abbey Gate, any assistance you know of?"

"Please send info," he responded. I did right away. It didn't take long before he responded back again that he had them added to their manifest.

"KAM Air 4420 is the next flight, and I'll be on it," Nick said, accompanied by a selfie of him on an empty plane headed to HKIA.

"Awesome," I wrote back. I knew a win like this would be added leverage to get in the gate.

After what seemed like a lifetime, I finally got a voice message from Abdul. They had made it to the airport without hitting any Taliban checkpoints. I allowed myself a small sigh of relief, and then immediately jumped on the NEO Comms to verify that the route was good for others to use. Abdul also told me the area around the gates was packed with people.

"Too much rush." he kept saying. "Keep trying to get to the front," I told him.

While the guys were fighting their way to the front of the gate, I reached out to Major Chris Davis. I heard that he had Marine and Special Ops contacts on the ground at Abbey Gate. Just like everyone else, he responded promptly. At this point, I'd heard his name a number of times, but hadn't communicated directly with him.

After a quick vetting session, he asked for all the guys' information and pictures to pass along to his team on the ground.

"I want to link them up with another family we think we're getting through shortly," he said. "This is going to work brother."

After a brief pause, Chris messaged again: "They are going to be contacted by a Tamim family. We are guiding them to your location now."

We began trading the pics that Abdul and the Tamim family were sending us to steer them together. It was 11:00 p.m. EST on Tuesday, August 24.

"I pray this works, I haven't slept in days," I told Chris. Everyone working on *#DigitalDunkirk* knew this was the final push, and we could sleep later. I was so buried in my phone and computer I barely came up for air. My girlfriend Ashlynn became worried about me. But, I knew I wouldn't be able to live with myself if I didn't do everything I could to get them out.

We came up with a code word so that Chris' Special Ops team could identify Abdul, Mohammad and their families. Abdul was able to find a small piece of cardboard and borrowed a marker from a fellow Afghan and wrote the word MARMAL on it. It was the NATO camp in Mazar-e Sharif where we had met what seemed like a lifetime ago.

I told him to hold the sign up for the Special Ops team to see, then passed the info along to Chris.

"They are holding up a sign that says Marmal as well as waving a white scarf."

"Keep them patient," Chris responded.

We had the two families continuously take and transmit photos, so we could pinpoint their location. We could tell from the photos that they were getting very close to each other. I was confident that the team would spot and gather them together in a matter of minutes.

"Break, Break, Break," the NEO chat read. "We have intel that a VBIED attack at HKIA is imminent."

This wasn't a surprise to any of us. The mass gathering of people and the chaos all around created the ideal environment for the sick and twisted mind of an ISIS-K zealot. Everyone knew that the risk was high, and the longer the operation went on, the higher it got.

But in terms of timing, it was devastating. We were so close to putting them under the protection of a U.S. Special Ops team. Once in their hands, I had no doubt they'd end up safely inside HKIA. Now, we were in limbo and they were still on their own.

The Roller Coaster Ride

For the next 45 minutes, Abdul and Mohammad went dark again. My mind ran free with all the possible things that might be happening to them during that time. None of them were good. It was now 12:15 a.m., Wednesday, August 25 and I could barely see straight from lack of sleep, not eating, staring glassy-eyed at my phone. Then I got a text from Abdul.

"We are in the airport now."

I fell over on the couch reading and rereading the message. We did it! They were in. I called Abdul, and had him put me on with the Marine he said was with him. His name was Desmond, but I wasn't able to catch his rank. I could hear absolute commotion on the other end of the call.

"This is Sergeant Mikael Cook, United States Army. I can personally vouch for these men, they are SIV and manifested on KAM Air Flight 4420."

"Roger, Sergeant, I'll get them down to State right now," he said.

I sat back in disbelief. I'm not too religious, but I felt that the hand of God must have gotten involved to make it all happen.

I messaged Chris Davis right away. "They just grabbed them, said they were taking them to the State Dept now."

"Fucking fantastic!" Chris replied.

I messaged Abdul. "Make sure you tell the State Dept you are manifested on KAM Air Flight 4420 to UAE."

Minutes later, I got a call on my cell from Abdul. I answered it thinking nothing but good news. They were on their way to the plane? They wanted me to send them photos of Michigan, where they would soon be living? The kids wanted to say thank you in broken English?

Wrong all the way around! They had been kicked back out of the airport because they were only SIV applicants and hadn't gotten their approval yet. Which, of course, can take years.

This was an absolute dagger to my heart. You could have run me over with a cement truck and it would have hurt less.

I couldn't even process the news. Human beings aren't wired to ride a roller coaster of emotions like this. My will almost collapsed at that moment. But, I finally pulled myself together and messaged Chris to tell him the news.

"What! Goddamnit," Davis replied.

I wanted to vent my own frustration and anger face to face with the person who made the decision to send them back out, but it was probably a nameless, faceless State Department employee. Desmond, the Marine, he was just following orders. I know it didn't bring him any pleasure.

In fact, when I talked to the 2/1 Marines later, they said that the absolute worst assignment was having to bring someone back out of HKIA because State Department officials turned them away. After experiencing the relief, maybe even exhilaration of getting through Abbey Gate and into the airport, they had their future snatched cruelly away right at the finish line. We heard stories of Afghans begging the Marines to shoot them rather than bring them back outside.

Davis messaged me again, "Keep attacking, this is going to work."

It was the exact message I needed to hear. I promised myself right then and there that I wasn't going to fucking quit until Abdul, Mohammad, and their families were on American soil.

I started going back through my contact list to see if I was missing anything. I was so invested in my conversation with Major Davis that I had over 100 missed texts. Thanks to the unnamed news organization leaking my number, I was still getting messages from Afghans asking for help. As heartbreaking as it was, I knew I had to keep my focus on Abdul and Mohammad.

As Tuesday night turned into Wednesday, August 25 in the U.S., a message came across NEO Comms: "ALCON: This is the situation at HKIA, Today is likely the last day of NEO recovery on HKIA, DoS has brokered a deal with TB to let only AMCITS through the HKIA Gate."

Quickly translated: "Our guys and the bad guys agreed that if you don't have a U.S. passport, you're up shit creek." Literally and figuratively.

Gabe, the group's leader, added, "Start getting emotionally prepared for the reality that we've done all we could do here, and to be frank, we've managed to save a lot of souls."

He was right. This group had saved a lot of lives over the past week. But not my guys.

I decided to message Kate at Barstool again as a last-ditch effort.

"Sorry for messaging again, one more try. My guys are right up front at the Abbey gate. They're on a flight manifest but still can't get in. Know anyone else?"

Kate responded right away. "Can I repost the above on insta with your handle so people can reach out to you if they can help? If not I totally understand. I'm afraid I'll fall asleep or be with my baby and miss someone who might be able to help."

"Yes please," I responded. A few minutes later the picture I had sent her of Abdul's position was posted on her and the *Zero Blog Thirty* Instagram page.

A half hour later, Kate messaged me with a link to the Instagram account of a woman named Avani. I messaged her right away and introduced myself. Little did I know, it would be the start of an intense working relationship that's morphed into a friendship between two people who traveled in very different circles—and definitely wouldn't have crossed paths any other way.

Her name is Avani Singh. She messaged me right back to tell me she was working with Allied Airlift21 helping to arrange flights out of HKIA. They had contacts at the gate, she said, and she forwarded Abdul and Mohammad's photos. It ended up going no further this time, but Avani and I would talk and text often in the weeks ahead.

While I was hitting the phones, Abdul and Mohammad were pushing back towards the front of the gate. After being kicked out of HKIA, they had every reason to have given up hope and gone home. But knowing that the situation in Kabul was getting more desperate and their families were depending on them, they had the incentive to keep trying.

WhatsApp wasn't working at this point, so Abdul was calling me on the main line to update me. Each time I would answer he would begin with the customary Afghan greeting, "Hello brother how is your family?"

"Abdul, stop asking me how my family is! Tell me what's going on!"

I could again hear the panic in the shouting voices in the background. "We are getting close to the U.S. forces," he told me.

"OK, get one of them to get on the phone with me." Then there was silence. The call dropped.

In Michigan, it was 5:00 a.m. on the 25th. In Kabul, it was 2:30 p.m. Chris Davis messaged me again. "Any update? Our teams lost comms with your guys because of the jammers."

As I was reading the message from Chris my phone rang again. The caller ID showed me it was Abdul.

"Abdul, where are you?" I asked. But he didn't have his phone to his ear. I could hear him yelling. From the volume of his voice I could tell that he was frantically trying to get someone's attention.

"Talk to the sergeant!" he was yelling. "Talk to the sergeant!"

I heard a muffled sound as the phone exchanged hands.

An unexpected voice came over the phone. "Sergeant Zielinski, United States Marines,"

I remember recoiling in surprise at hearing an American voice, then quickly recovering.

"Sergeant Cook. United States Army," I replied. "These men are SIV visa holders. I worked with them in Mazar-e Sharif. I have them manifested on KAM Air Flight 4420 and have them on the USFOR-A-FWD Evac roster. Please let them in."

"I don't see their visas here," he replied.

"Brother, please," I begged him. "They're my friends and they're going to get killed."

There was a brief pause. The silence felt heavy with the weight of those words. It was the first time I recall saying that aloud.

Finally, Zielenski said, "OK, I'll let them through but you have to come down here and escort them to State."

My heart sank again. He thought I was boots on the ground at the airport.

"I'm stateside." I said. "I have no one that can escort them. Can you please have one of your guys take them down?"

"Alright, I'll pull one of my guys and have them escorted down, I can't promise they will make it through State though."

"Understood, thank you brother," I responded.

Then he asked, "Is it just this one family?"

"No, there's another family behind them and a brother."

"OK, roger," he replied. And then the call was disconnected.

I slumped back on the couch in disbelief, then rolled my neck slowly to try and release the tension that had me seized in an iron grip. I ran the conversation through my head. Did that just happen?

They were in again. I was relieved, but I remembered we had been here before and it didn't work out. For the next two hours, there was nothing but silence. I saw slivers of the sunrise come through my shades and I levitated in that strange void between wake and sleep. I got up and went to my bed to try and sleep, but couldn't. I was exhausted beyond any measure, but too hyper-alert to give in to it.

At 7:08 a.m. EST, my phone pinged. I shot up like I had been electrocuted and looked at a photo Abdul had texted me, then blinked and refocused my eyes to make sure what I thought I saw was accurate. It was a selfie of Abdul wearing a State Dept. bracelet and a weary smile. Mohammad and other family members crowded around him. They made it! They were officially inside and safe.

I was euphoric when I messaged Chris Davis. "They're all in, can't thank you enough."

"Team wins," he responded. "You're a stud, thanks for trusting the process, and remaining steadfast in your convictions. This shit has been so taxing."

While I appreciated his comments. I knew it was a group effort. So many people had worked to get us to this point. Every effort by every person involved pushed the needle in the right direction. I've never witnessed a truer display of teamwork.

It would be a while before I learned the true impact and scope of #DigitalDunkirk. I learned recently that Major Davis, for example, is credited with helping to evacuate 500 Afghan allies over the course of the operation, including the nine family members who put their blind trust in me. I was a very small cog in a very big machine.

The reward? Abdul called me to thank me for my help.

"I wish my English was better so I could tell you how thankful I am brother." Needless to say, the emotion that moment produced is something I'll never forget.

In the midst of the celebration, there was a setback. Abdul's younger brother, Massoud, wasn't able to get in. The Marines had let Abdul's and Mohammad's families in, but in the mayhem didn't realize that Massoud was also a part of the group. Abdul is very close to him, and it was a major disappointment, but we had to keep moving forward.

He followed up by sending me a group photo of all of them in the airport waiting on their plane. Looking at them in the airport hangar, I could see the exhaustion etched in their faces. Two men, two women and five children under the age of eight—hungry, thirsty, fearful of the barbarians who wanted to enslave them, forced to stand in sewage water for days just trying to get past a gate to save their lives. As an American, it's hard to even fathom that we put them in that position, and that so many of them were going to get left behind.

I ended up forwarding it to Kate at *Zero Blog Thirty* to express my gratitude for her help. I can't imagine how many messages flooded her inbox, yet she was always there for me immediately whenever I asked for her help.

"They're fucking in, all 9, thanks to you," I told her.

She replied minutes later. "Holy shit, don't even have the words. You didn't give up and there they are. Going to sound incredibly dorky but proud of you and the lengths you went to."

Over nine hours after getting through the gate, the guys sent me a picture of them getting on the plane. This is where it finally got real for me. I got up off the couch, walked upstairs to my room and threw both my fists in the air. I was alone in my room, fist pumping and clapping. We did it! We all did it together!

I reached back out to Nick Palmisciano to let him know the good news. "Fuck yeah, so happy for you," he replied.

Shortly after I got a message from Gabe, the leader of the NEO Comms chat. News traveled fast in the chat room.

"Heard you got your people out. You did it dude. Proud of you and everyone else who stepped up and made shit happen."

It obviously couldn't have happened without his leadership, so I replied, "What a community we have, took a shit ton of people."

But the job wasn't done yet. All the high fives were a little premature, like celebrating a game-tying goal to force overtime. It wouldn't be a win until we got them on the ground in the States.

The next day, August 26 at 3:30 a.m. EST, Abdul messaged me a picture of them in Qatar at a military installation. They were officially safe from Taliban reach. I told them to get some rest and I would figure out the next steps to try to get them to the United States. At that late stage in the evacuation process, tens of thousands of Afghans were in "lily pad" locations in over a dozen countries, including thousands at Ramstein Air Base in Germany, and many more scattered from Italy to Albania, Denmark, Tajikistan, Bahrain and many more countries around the globe.

While anywhere was better than Afghanistan, I wanted to try and avoid having them get wrapped in a red-tape nightmare in some remote location. Like Albania, for example, where four months later, 1,000 Afghans were still stuck at a hotel in an off-season resort town, far from the chaos of their home, but no closer to their final destination.[4]

---

4   Aljazeera, 12/21/21.

Much as we wanted them here ASAP, I finally had to give in to exhaustion. I could barely form a thought at that point and wouldn't be of any help to them, so I decided to get a few hours of sleep knowing they were safe. Aside from one-eye-open catnaps, it had been a few days since I had really slept at all.

I woke up around 8:00 a.m. and sat back down at my computer to try and get some work done. Believe it or not, I still had a job. I can't thank my employer, FastenMaster, and my boss, Nikki Long, enough for allowing me to take the time to help Abdul and Mohammad. She took on my workload while I stayed engaged with the evacuation. As you can see from all the texts, those of us directly involved got all the credit, but there was a much wider community of people and organizations who made it possible.

With pages of work-related emails in front of me, I took a deep breath and readied myself to get back into work mode. And then I heard the familiar NEO Comms chat notification firing off. This time, it didn't seem to stop.

CHAPTER 11

The Blast

"Break Break Break. Explosion at Abbey Gate confirmed US casualties."

Reading that, I felt like I had been kicked in the stomach. I put my head on the table and said a prayer. Then I remembered Abdul's brother, Massoud. Had he gone back to the gate in an effort to get out on his own? Without telling Abdul what had happened, I sent him a message asking if he had heard from his brother. No, he replied, he hadn't.

As I waited for more news about the severity of the blast and the number of casualties, my thoughts turned to Sergeant Zielinski and the Marines at the gate. I prayed he wasn't on duty when the explosion occurred.

But I knew from seeing the photos and hearing the voicemails from Abdul that there would be a significant loss of life if the explosion happened near the gate. It was packed with humanity and surrounded by concrete walls that would contain and amplify the blast. There were going to be grieving family members and friends all across the world by the time the day was done. I was sure of that.

Just over 45 minutes after the initial message, another came across: "Confirmed 12 DoD casualties" (this would later get increased to 13).

I broke down and wept like a baby at my desk. Ashlynn came over and hugged me from behind. I was so distraught, I couldn't even say anything. All I could think about were the families of the U.S. service members who were killed. They were probably at work, drinking coffee, shooting the shit with colleagues, with hardly a care in the world.

By lunchtime, they would have found out that their son or daughter, husband or wife was gone forever. By dinner, their kids, sisters, brothers and extended families would hear the news. Shock, disbelief, and finally grief, would spill out into their communities, and their lives would never, ever, be the same again.

For the 2/1 Marines who survived the explosion, that's the feeling they carry to this day. In addition to carrying around the burden of survivor's guilt, they lost friends and brothers, and something else they'll never get back.

"Part of me got left behind in Afghanistan that day and will never return," Sergeant Williamson explains.

As I sat overcome with emotion at my desk, I wasn't aware of the estimated 160 to 170 Afghan civilians who lost their lives at the gate that day also. They too, would have families who would grieve. The fact that they are more used to grief than we are doesn't make their pain any less. The Afghan lives lost that day are no less important than the American ones.

For 2/1 Marines, August 26 was a day that began like the others at Abbey Gate: a blurred collage of desperation and chaos. They rotated in and out of shifts at the outer gate, alongside the canal, or at the inner gate as a designated QRF (Quick Reaction Force) team. On command orders, they had taken a knee behind jersey barriers due to enhanced SVIED threats (suicide vest IED) from nearly midnight on the 25th to sunrise on the morning of the 26th.

By this time, crowds in just the canal area alone had increased to an estimated 10,000, while thousands more packed the gate areas. They were "noticeably more desperate," the CENTCOM report notes. Whether they were aware of the Pentagon plans to shut down the gates due to the enhanced threats is unclear. But they were aware the clock was ticking, and their demeanor showed it.

Late in the afternoon of the 25th, 2/1 Marines' Echo Company and British 2nd PARA linked up and pushed the crowd back 150 yards from the base of the sniper tower, but concerns about the units being overextended and exposed to an SVIED attack forced them to collapse their position back to where they started.

The feeling that an attack by ISIS was coming wasn't a matter of if, but when, and it wasn't only felt on the ground at HKIA. Back at the Pentagon on the morning of the 25th, Defense Secretary Lloyd Austin had instructed a dozen or so of the DoD's top leadership to prepare for an imminent mass casualty attack at HKIA. There was significant U.S. intelligence that ISIS-K was preparing a complex attack, according to classified documents obtained by the news site, Politico.[1]

Based on that assessment, Rear Admiral Vasely, a former Navy SEAL officer and commander of Special Operations Joint Task Force—Afghanistan, then scheduled to shut Abbey Gate at 6:00 p.m. on the 25th, but according to CENTCOM, that order was postponed because the UK's 2nd PARA still needed to process 1,000 evacuees from the Baron Hotel through the inner gate.

Plans to shut it again the morning of the 26th were shelved for the same reason, according to CENTCOM. But UK officials have since disputed their findings, saying that the decision to keep the gates open was consensual, and wasn't due to the UK's inability to process their evacuees in time to close them before the blast.[2]

Whatever the case, Abbey Gate stayed open as the main operating gate at HKIA. As the crowds increased, so did the efficiency of the evacuation process. Despite the security challenges, the numbers of people being evacuated kept rising. From an early average of 7,500 per day, the numbers spiked as high as 21,700 by the 26th.[3]

Zielinski recalls that day as another in a blur of chaotic days since his unit had deployed to the gate a week earlier. But there were noticeable differences. The crowds had grown larger and more frantic, and the bomb threats more frequent.

His Weapons Company squad was supposed to man the outer gate through the afternoon into the evening, but it was pulled out of the rotation in mid-afternoon and told to withdraw back to the inner gate and assemble as the QRF team.

Corporal Moore's Golf Company, 4th Platoon had worked a 12-hour shift along the canal and outer corridor, so at about 4:00 p.m. the decision was made to rotate them out and replace them with the company's

---

1 Politico, 8/30/21.
2 *The Guardian*, 8/31/21.
3 *Military Times*, 8/11/22.

1st Platoon. He went with the other members of his platoon to take a breather and eat an MRE back at the inner gate.

Sergeant Williamson was already back there, as were Lance Corporal Bair and Sergeant Ramirez. They had taken their Kevlar vests off and were "just shooting the shit and catching our breath," Zielinski recalls. It seemed like an ordinary moment at Abbey Gate, with the "structured and predictable battle rhythm" that CENTCOM described in its report.

Brigadier General Sullivan arrived at Abbey Gate just after 5:00 p.m. to discuss a new gate closure timeline with 2/1 Marines' company commanders. He left at approximately 5:15 p.m., just a few minutes before Army Staff Sergeant Ryan Knauss of the 9th Psychological Operations Battalion corralled an Afghan interpreter and gave him a bullhorn to urge the Afghans to stop pushing because there were children and women who were being crushed by the crowd.

It didn't work. By 5:30 p.m., most of Golf Company's 1st Platoon had consolidated at the base of the sniper tower to prevent a breach from the canal through the outer gate. Sergeant Knauss and his PSYOP truck were parked there as well.

Staff Sergeant Darin Hoover of 2/1's Echo Company was escorting an Afghan interpreter to look for his father right near the outer gate.

Sergeant Nicole Gee of 24th Marine Expeditionary Unit—whose image of her cradling an Afghan baby in her arms earlier in the week had gone viral around the world—was holding the line at the base of the sniper tower next to Sergeant Johnny Rosario-Pichardo of 5th Marine Expeditionary Brigade. Cognizant of cultural sensitivities, the Marines made sure there were females available to interact, and if necessary, search, female Afghans and children.

Just in front of them, Corporal Hunter Lopez, Corporal Daegan Page, Corporal Humberto Sanchez, Lance Corporal David Espinoza and Lance Corporal Jared Schmitz, all Golf Company Marines, were pushing back against the increasingly agitated crowd.

Lance Corporal Rylee McCollum, Lance Corporal Dylan Merola and Lance Corporal Kareem Nikoui, all also Golf Company Marines, stood on the wall above the canal. Photos taken that day showed Afghan civilians pressed shoulder to shoulder, back to chest in the canal as far as the eye could see. Almost all were holding up documents of some kind for the Marines to look at.

Navy Corpsman, HM3 Maxton Soviak, who was attached to Golf Company, was crouched next to the fence alongside the canal tending to an Afghan civilian who had collapsed from heat stroke.

At 5:36 p.m., a Marine standing approximately 52 yards back from the base of the sniper tower was filming on his phone when a figure dressed in all black briefly emerged from the crowd on the walkway on the far side of the canal. In a nanosecond, the figure was vaporized in a bright flash, and then clouds of smoke and debris filled the screen.

Al-Loghri, the ISIS-K bomber who had escaped from the Bagram prison, had detonated a 20lb SVIED packed with military-grade plastic explosive and thousands of 5mm (.2in) ball bearings. He was standing approximately 10 feet from the three Marines standing on the opposite canal wall. They never stood a chance.

Neither did the Marines clustered under the sniper tower, Hoover, over near the gate, Soviak, crouched near the fence, Knauss, standing on the passenger side of the PSYOP truck, or the approximately 160 to 170 Afghans standing in proximity to the blast. A DoD briefing on the release of the CENTCOM reported that the furthest of the 13 KIA U.S. service members was Knauss, who was 17 yards away from the point of detonation.

The reaction of the 2/1 Weapons Company Marines back at the inner gate was instantaneous: no time to think, just react.

"When the bomb went off I felt this massive vibration in my body," Williamson recalls. "Then it was pure reaction. We immediately threw on our Kevlars and ran down to the spot. That's when I saw things I will never forget as long as I live."

I've debated whether to leave out some of the descriptions the Marines gave of the aftermath of the explosion, but decided to put them in to avoid the all-too-common practice of sterilizing war and combat and making it seem like a *Call of Duty* video instead of the blood-and-guts horror it really is.

"Guys were walking around like zombies covered in blood. There were smoking body parts everywhere. There was brain matter on the

C-wire and the canal water had turned from brown to red," Williamson recounts.

Ramirez explains he ran to the CCP to help with the casualties, but his captain told him to get down to the site and provide security in case it was a coordinated attack.

"It was brutal to see. I remember I was calm, but like I was out of my body and could lose it at any second. I took a knee next to Corporal Lopez to see if I could help him. He had this look of shock and surprise on his face, so I thought he was alive. But when we got him onto a litter, his head rolled and I saw the same look on his face. Then I knew he was dead."

Zielinski says he and his team immediately ran to the site to help evacuate casualties back to the CCP. 2/1 Marines had undergone extensive CLS (Combat Lifesaver) training in Kuwait prior to the deployment to HKIA, and he attributes that training to lives being saved that day at Abbey Gate.

While he was sifting through the chaos at the site, he knelt to the ground and felt something underneath his right knee. He looked down to see an Army-issue multicam kevlar kit pinned under his knee. Later, Zielinski would realize it was Sergeant Knauss' kit.

Moore's 4th Platoon had just finished their 12-hour shift and were resting about 30 yards back from the sniper tower next to some vehicles when the bomb exploded.

"I saw body parts fly 15 to 20 feet in the air. Some ball bearings had hit the CS tear gas canisters Marines had on their belts, and clouds of tear gas and smoke were everywhere. It was absolute chaos."

He remembers grabbing an Army soldier who was staggering around dazed with a wounded arm and putting a tourniquet on him as he took in the scenes of carnage and devastation around him.

"I was in a zone. I saw wounded buddies down, but I wasn't really emotionally registering what I saw. I was just full of adrenaline."

After helping get the wounded back to the CCP, he helped lift McCollum's body onto the back of a Gator ATV. That wasn't the only KIA he recognized. He was good friends with most of Golf Company's dead, he said.

Though he was in another company, Williamson knew Hoover, Lopez and Page. Hoover, he said, had been helpful to him when he got his sergeant stripes. Zielinski also recalls working with Hoover during training.

Shortly after the blast, Williamson took a head count of his squad and came up one short. After searching frantically, but not finding him, he resorted to looking at all the Marine casualties to see if he was one of them.

"I was freaking out, but it turns out that he had been ordered back to the rear at the inner gate and didn't tell me. It's not really his fault in those circumstances, but it really fucked me up to have to look at all the KIAs' faces up close like that."

In addition to the 13 KIA, 45 American service members were wounded that day. Had it not been for the Marines' CLS training, the incredible work of the Navy corpsmen at the explosion site, and the work of trauma and surgical teams back inside the airport, and later in Germany and stateside, many more could have easily been KIA.

A month before ceding control of Bagram Air Base to the ANA in July, the Pentagon had transferred its medical facility—the best in Afghanistan—to HKIA. Complete with two operating rooms, and laboratory and imaging machines, it was supplemented by the arrival of nine U.S., UK and Norwegian surgical teams between August 20 and 23.

Twelve minutes after the blast, the facility received the first of the 27 wounded U.S. troops it would treat before they were evacuated to Germany. One of those was Tyler Vargas-Andrews, a 24-year-old Weapons Company squad leader. He was so grievously wounded, Williamson recalls thinking there was no way he'd survive.

"I remember seeing him getting dragged to the CCP on a riot shield and thinking I'd never see him again."

Vargas-Andrews lost his right arm and left leg, had a lacerated liver, a hole in his bladder and ended up having 43 surgeries before he was discharged from Walter Reed Hospital nearly a year after the blast. The medical intervention he received at HKIA saved his life.

Another casualty was Corporal Wyatt Wilson (promoted in 2022 to sergeant), a team leader in Golf Company who was positioned 10 yards from the bomb when it detonated. Wilson was thrown in the air by the blast and the ball-bearing shrapnel tore through his body.

Despite life-threatening wounds, he dragged Corporal Kelsee Lainhart, another seriously wounded Marine, away from the blast site towards the CCP, stopping only when he was able to hand her off to an uninjured Marine. Corporal Lainhart was left paralyzed from the injuries she received in the explosion.

Wilson then waved off medical treatment for himself and went back to help others, before he was finally convinced to let a corpsman attend to him and get him to the HKIA medical facility. For his heroics, he was awarded the Bronze Star with the V device for valor.

In addition to the 27 wounded U.S. service members treated that day, 18 more would be diagnosed after the deployment with TBI (Traumatic Brain Injury) or concussions.

In the immediate aftermath of the explosion, the crackle of small-arms fire shattered the concussive silence that the bomb produced. Although the reports of gunfire aren't disputed by the authors of the CENTCOM report, the origin and intent are.

The day of the bombing, Pentagon press secretary Admiral John Kirby called it a "complex attack," indicating the command at HKIA believed that ISIS-K had planned and executed an attack involving the bomber Al-Loghri with his SVIED and gunmen around the perimeter.

By the time the report was issued six months later, CENTCOM had backed off that assertion and spent a good amount of time disputing that claim. The gunfire, it determined, was a combination of warning shots fired by UK and U.S. troops after the blast.

In summarizing over 100 interviews it conducted with U.S. military personnel on the ground at HKIA, the report claims that the only ones who reported incoming gunfire were Marines who "were exhausted, were experiencing sensory overload... and were within the blast zone and suffered potential TBIs or concussions from the event."

However, it's the next point that some of the 2/1 Marines I spoke with were most upset about. "It is worth noting that the only Marines who reported receiving fire following the explosion were junior Marines with no prior combat experience," the report concluded.

Williamson, for one, is adamant that 2/1 Marines were taking incoming fire immediately after the explosion and he's not shy about saying it. He watched rounds kicking up dirt at his feet after the bomb and could hear them hitting objects around him, he claims. They couldn't be mistaken for anything else, he argues, especially well after the bomb had expelled the ball bearings.

"My motivation to speak out for this book is to honor my brother Marines who died there, but it's also to correct the misinformation. They said there were no rounds being fired at us. That's bullshit! There were gunshot wound victims. Some of the doctors said so. Lots of Marines know this, but they're making it like we misjudged what was happening because we didn't have combat experience. I don't know why. But it's wrong!"

There are plenty of others in the public forum who dispute the CENTCOM findings, so he's not alone in that assessment. If true, it's hard to rationalize why the Pentagon would deny it. The only reason I can think of is they might not want to give ISIS-K any more PR ammunition for attacking and killing U.S. service members than they already had.

Some speculate that the Taliban might have taken advantage of the chaos to take some free shots at exposed U.S. troops. There's no proof of that, but there's plenty of evidence that the Taliban took great delight in "actively taunting the Marines," as the report points out. "They were constantly testing the waters with us to see what they could get away with," Zielinski recalls.

Williamson says he happened to look over at the Chevron after the explosion and saw a number of Taliban soldiers standing on the shipping containers jeering and laughing.

"It was like being back in high school and seeing some guy slip and fall in the hallway and everyone laughing at him," he remembers, his voice laced with venom.

The issue of whether it was a coordinated attack will never be fully resolved, and it's a footnote to the bigger picture of what happened that day. But details matter to the troops who manned Abbey Gate, because it's the details—the intense green of a girl's eyes, the indescribable smell that soaked into their pores, the death mask of surprise on a brother Marine's face—that will stay with them for a long, long, time.

As devastating as the explosion was to the service members at Abbey Gate, we can't ever forget the price paid by the Afghan civilians who were there. The fact that we still have only an estimate of the number of deaths they suffered that day and no idea of the wounded speaks to the extent of that price.

I'm aware of the number of times I've referred to the "desperate crowd" at Abbey Gate, which I've resorted to as a way to describe the atmosphere that existed. But, I'm also aware that it can have the effect of dehumanizing them and robbing them of their own personal stories. We can't ever forget that everyone there that day had one.

Like Najma Sadeqi, a beautiful 20-year-old Kabul resident. She was a journalism student who had been featured on a YouTube channel portraying the life of young Afghans. Smart, curious and vivacious, Najma and her videos had amassed a large following prior to the Taliban takeover.

Four days after Kabul fell, she recorded her last video from inside her family's home. The colorful clothing of her earlier videos had been replaced by a full-length traditional black tunbaan and chador to cover her head. She was saying goodbye to her audience. The Taliban had promised women and girls would be able to attend school and go to work, but she didn't believe them. She had already received threatening phone calls and text messages telling her to stop with her videos.

"I wish this was all a bad dream we could wake up from," she said with tears in her eyes. "But I know the reality is we are finished." A week later, she went to HKIA with her brother and cousin in an effort to get out. She was clutching printouts of the threatening messages she received from the Taliban to show the Marines at Abbey Gate when the bomb went off. All three of them were killed.[4]

Or Mohammed Niazi, an immigrant from Kabul who had settled in Farnborough, England when he was a teenager. He went back to Kabul with his wife and three-year-old daughter in an effort to get the rest of

---

4   CNN, 8/31/21.

his family out. All three were killed in the explosion. They left three other children behind.[5]

My friends, Abdul, Mohammad and their families got lucky. Najma, Mohammed and their families did not. Sergeant Zielinski, Sergeant Williamson, Sergeant Ramirez, Corporal Moore and Lance Corporal Bair got lucky. The 13 U.S. service members who were killed that day did not.

A few yards left or right, a few minutes before or after, the right color document at the right time; the hand of fate dealt some cruel cards at Abbey Gate.

---

5   BBC, 8/31/21.

CHAPTER 12

The Mission Continues— The Paiman Rescue

Abdul, Mohammad and their families fled Kabul with literally just the clothes on their backs. As I decompressed in the immediate aftermath of their escape, my thoughts turned to phase two, which was getting them the things they would need to begin a new life here in America.

As they left Qatar for another flight to the U.S. Army base in Kaiserslautern, Germany, Ashlynn put together a list of things they would need and registered it on Amazon. We also started a GoFundMe campaign for them called #OperationJustOneMore. Within 24 hours, the incredible generosity of people who responded had provided for every item on the Amazon wish list, and we ultimately raised over $15,000 on GoFundMe.

Without knowing how long they would be in Germany, I decided to pack up a couple of suitcases of clothes and try to get myself on a military flight to Kaiserslautern. So, I reached out to my chain of command to see about getting on a Space A flight. For anyone not familiar with the terminology, Space A refers to "Space Available." One of the best perks of the military is the ability for any active duty service member to jump on a military flight to almost anywhere in the world if there's an empty seat available.

The first stop on the chain was Sergeant First Class David Zeleny, who we all referred to as Sergeant Z. He led my platoon during our deployment and is highly respected by every member of our unit. He also knew and liked Abdul and Mohammad. When I gave him a summary of their escape, he was blown away, and his reaction was appreciative, and typically unfiltered.

He kicked my request up the line to our company commander, Captain Kimmelman, another unit member who was highly respected by all for her leadership and no bullshit attitude.

The next morning I got a call back from Sergeant Z. In the course of the call, he said that the news about my involvement in *#DigitalDunkirk* had spread fast, and that a company commander of another unit in our battalion had a soldier whose family was currently stuck in Afghanistan and couldn't get out. He wanted to know if I could help them.

To be honest, I did hesitate. I was still exhausted from the previous week of little sleep, and I was trying to catch up with my life—with my girlfriend, my job, my family. I honestly thought I was one and done in the Afghan evacuation business.

But as I was thinking this, an internal dialogue drowned out that voice. It went something like this—"He's a United States soldier, he's in your unit, and his family is still there, for fuck's sake! What would happen to them if the Taliban finds out?!"

So, I told Sergeant Z to have the company commander call me and give me the details. Even though it was very late in the game, I had to at least try to help.

As I waited for the call, another call came in from Germany. Abdul, Mohammad and their families had landed safely. They had been given a backpack of clothes and basic necessities, Abdul told me, and were being fed and housed. He handed the phone over to a soldier, who told me that they would most likely be there for 10 days before boarding a flight to the U.S. I was grateful they ended up at a U.S. Army base in Germany rather than in a remote location like Albania.

The next morning, I received the call I was waiting for from Captain Minnich, the commander of the 983rd Forward Support Company. I had never talked to him before, but we had passed each other in the hallways many times before. After a little more small talk, we got down to the issue at hand.

One of the enlisted men in his unit, Specialist Bismillah Paiman, had grown up in Afghanistan, and would later serve as an interpreter for U.S. troops. Because of that service, he was able to get a green card and come to the U.S. On arrival, he then decided to enlist in the Army. He was grateful to his new country and proud to serve as an American soldier.

Like so many Afghans though, he paid the personal price of leaving his family behind. Now, with the Taliban in power, his family—mother, sister and three brothers—would be at great risk if that fact was revealed. It was bad enough that he was a former interpreter. To have a family member serving as an active-duty U.S. soldier; that could be an automatic death sentence!

If that wasn't dangerous enough for them, he and his family were Hazara, an ethnic minority who have been persecuted in Afghanistan and neighboring Pakistan for centuries, especially by the Pashtun, who make up the traditional base of the Taliban. An estimated 10 percent of Afghanistan's 40 million people are of Hazara descent.[1]

Said to originally be descendants of Genghis Khan, the Hazara have Mongolian features and speak Dari, the same as Abdul and Mohammad and most of Kabul's residents, but different from the Taliban's Pashto. In addition, they are also minority Shi'a Muslims, while Taliban are majority Sunni.

Learning about the Hazara's tortured history makes you want to quit the human race. Over the centuries, they've been brutalized, butchered, enslaved and driven into exile by the millions. In the late 1800s, Afghanistan's leader, Emir Abdur Rahman Khan, was known for the sadistic delight he took in almost wiping them off the map.

He wasn't the first, and unfortunately, isn't the last. In 1998, the Taliban killed thousands of them in Mazar-e Sharif in a bloody week-long massacre. It was said they drove through the narrow streets of the city and went house to house seeking out and killing Hazara men, boys, even infants.[2]

Their lives improved when the U.S. and coalition forces arrived, and the Taliban were driven out of power. They won the right to vote, and even ended up winning 25 percent of the seats in the Afghan parliament

---

1   Voice of America, 5/6/22.
2   *Sunday Times*, 11/1/98.

by 2010. The violence against them never stopped, but the widespread systematic slaughter did.

But in the lead-up to the 2021 Taliban takeover, the Hazara were once again targeted. Not only by the Taliban, but by ISIS too, who have a rabid hatred of Shi'a. For instance, ISIS targeted a Hazara wedding in Kabul with a bomb in 2019, killing 63 guests.

The following year, they sprayed automatic weapons fire at a memorial commemoration of a Hazara leader, killing 32 people, and then followed that up by attacking a maternity hospital in Kabul, killing 24, including two newborns.

In May, 2021, as the Taliban were beginning their march to take over the country, one of the two groups bombed a girls' school in a predominantly Hazara neighborhood in West Kabul, killing 90 schoolgirls.[3] The Taliban denied responsibility for the despicable attack, and ISIS never claimed it. Even terrorist groups know the damage that can result from very bad PR.

The brutality against the Hazara continues unabated to this day. Amnesty International issued a report in August, 2022 citing the killing of over 100 Hazara civilians by ISIS-K in West Kabul in just the month prior. They urged the Taliban to provide security to protect them. Which is like asking the fox to watch over the chicken coop. Meanwhile, the Hazaras' only crime is to have been born.

I told Captain Minnich I would do everything I could to help, and then immediately started sending him all the documents I knew needed to be filled out to try and get the Paiman family on a DoD evacuation list and get them manifested on a flight out.

I also added Captain Minnich to the NEO Comms chat group so he could see and actively engage in the process firsthand. Then I reached back out to the contacts I had previously made to try and get fresh intel about the conditions at HKIA now that Abbey Gate had been closed. It felt like I had left a party, gone for a walk around the block, and came back in the door again to see the same familiar faces and a few newcomers.

---

3 *New York Times*, 5/16/21.

By the morning of the next day, August 27, I hadn't developed any promising leads. But with the deadline closing in three days, we had to be ready at a moment's notice, so I suggested to Minnich that he tell the family to get to the airport. They had traveled from their hometown of Ghazni, and were holed up in a house in Kabul.

Soon after, a warning came over the NEO Comms chat. "Break Break Break★★★★WARNING★★★★High confidence unclass report 7 suicide bombers just left Abdul Rahman Mosque. Headed to HKIA. Moments ago from CIA."

I forwarded the message to Minnich to make sure he saw it. "Last time we got this warning, it was true," I told him. "I'll keep looking for options, but you may want to move them away safely."

"I just heard they closed the airport and only AMCITS now," he wrote.

While I wasn't sure that was the case at that moment, I wasn't ready to throw in the towel either. I'd heard of a number of Special Ops guys who had established "ratlines"—secret routes that allowed small escorted groups to gain access into HKIA. We just had to find out where they were and who was running them.

As we were attempting to do just that, we received a message that an outsider had infiltrated our chat room and was picking up on the intel we were sharing. It was unclear if the outsider was Taliban or Pakistan's intel agency ISI. The chat leader called for an immediate shutdown of the Signal chat, and then created a smaller group with much tighter vetting. Not many people are aware that the Taliban have become pretty tech savvy since the days we first heard of them hiding in caves from B-52 bombers back in 2001. The new chat room name was AFG Phase II Landing Zone.

I decided to reach back out to Avani Singh at Allied Airlift21 and let her know about this new mission. When she responded, I found out that—like just about everyone involved in *#DigitalDunkirk*—she had just finished her own week-long operation and was exhausted herself.

Avani is one of the more memorable connections I made during my involvement in the HKIA evacuation. One reason was simply that we ended up spending a ton of time working on this Paiman evacuation together over the next month. Any relationship forged in the heat of battle is bound to be stronger. We remain good friends to this day.

But even more so, she is a force of nature who demands equal justice for all and won't take no for an answer. You can try, but you won't get far, trust me. The daughter of Indian immigrants, Avani grew up in New Jersey and moved to the Washington D.C. area to attend undergraduate school at George Washington University.

On August 15, Avani had just started a new job at a Capital One after a career as a federal consultant at Deloitte and an internship at the State Department, when a friend sent her a message asking if she knew anyone who could get some close family friends out of Kabul.

The request resonated with her, Avani says, because her grandfather had to leave his homeland after the 1947 partition dividing the Indian subcontinent into Muslim-majority Pakistan and Hindu-majority India. A native Punjabi Sikh, he died in March, 2021 without ever having returned home. She knew from him how traumatic forced exile could be on a person, and she felt she had to help.

She messaged some people she knew at the State Department about her friend's family, and was eventually told they would be put on a list that they were compiling of high-value evacuees. It turns out that the woman in the family was a former adviser to the first lady of Afghanistan. They eventually would get a visa to the UK. Avani wasn't sure if her involvement helped, but the fact that it happened piqued her interest.

Soon after, a neighbor from New Jersey mentioned that she had an Afghan friend who had trained with the New Jersey National Guard and was now stuck in Kabul and desperate to get out. Avani decided to jump in with both feet, and soon, she had connected with Allied Airlift21. From that point on, she was all-in on the *#DigitalDunkirk* mission. She eventually became a caseworker for the organization.

When I reached out to Avani and told her it involved the family of a U.S. Army soldier, she decided she would sleep when she was dead and switched instantly into her high-energy, action-hero mode. We started scouring sources and bouncing ideas with each other about how to get the Paiman family out through the narrowing window that was left.

Avani had developed a previous contact with "PK," an Army Ranger veteran who had contacts with ratlines into HKIA, and was still going outside the wire to bring small groups into the airport. She managed to get a hold of him, and he reluctantly agreed to allow us to add the Paimans to his list. At that point, with the gates closed, I'm sure he was being hounded left and right to get people in, so it was a major coup to get him to agree to bring them along.

I contacted Captain Minnich to let him know, and then started a new Signal chat with Minnich, Avani and Bismillah Paiman, who we referred to as "B" during the operation. In short order, we were then added to an operations chat called AA21+PK, which consisted of military Special Ops forces, CIA officers, and other DoD officials who were acting as case managers to extract high-value Afghans—and some Americans—the government hadn't yet managed to exfiltrate. It was definitely the big leagues.

"We have 20 hours to get people out," PK wrote in the chat. I thought of the Army saying, "Slow is smooth, smooth is fast." I knew it was probably going to go down to the wire and we were in for another long night.

Shortly after, we received a pin on a map of HKIA and the surrounding area indicating where the Paiman family needed to go. It was located at the southwest side of the airport, next to the Mumtaz Mahal Wedding Hall, one of the giant, garishly lit, Las Vegas-style wedding venues that light up the horizon in the urban areas of the country.

This "ratline" didn't have a name, but it was a potential way into the airport. The Paimans had 30 minutes to get there, the message said. We relayed the information to "B" and asked him to do whatever he had to do to guide the family to this location. Incredibly, they were close by and immediately responded that they could get there in time.

In the interim, Avani and I worked feverishly to get all the necessary paperwork in order to facilitate the process once they got there. Avani then sent the family a video of a red and white barrier gate that had been knocked down and lay on the ground at the X spot. This, she told them, was exactly where they needed to be for the snatch-and-grab operation PK had drawn up.

After a few lost-in-translation exchanges between us, "B," and his family, they sent us photos of their surroundings, and we were able to determine they were in the right spot. Night had fallen in Kabul, and the family was getting nervous. Avani and I could feel their tension from our locations in Virginia and Michigan.

I felt my own tension ease somewhat when the family told us they saw U.S. soldiers escorting a group of people into HKIA, but shortly after it spiked again when PK sent a message over the chat accompanied by a new pin on a map.

"I need everyone to move their families to this new location for safety reasons."

The new location was the Panjshir gas station at the far northern perimeter of the airport. The gate there was named Glory Gate by some, Liberty Gate by others, and was run by CIA operatives. The CIA-trained Afghan paramilitary unit known as 02 was assisting with security there.[4]

PK instructed us to have the families move in small groups, but to maintain visual contact with each other while they did. My heart skipped a few beats when I read this. It was very dangerous for anyone to be moving around at night outside HKIA, let alone a family with the kind of baggage the Paimans had.

"B" relayed the news to his family, and then Avani and I made small talk with him while they traveled to keep us all distracted from the danger they were in. Just over 30 minutes later the family sent us a picture of the gas station. They made it! It was after midnight in Kabul.

As they were en route, I noticed in the chat forum that some people were communicating directly with the White House. *How the hell did I end up in here? I do not have the security clearance for this.* At this point, #DigitalDunkirk was like a Wild West town under siege. If you were useful somehow, you got a deputy's badge and were put to work.

PK then forwarded a text from the exfiltration team on the ground who were working the operation.

"My team is hoping to get you through to HKIA tonight, while we can't promise anything. Please make your way to the following gas station and standby. I will also need the following: 1, I need a picture of your entire group 2, drop a pin of your location 3, need all names 4, you should hold up this photo on your phone if anyone asks for a photo verification."

---

4   *Wall Street Journal*, 10/14/21.

Attached to the text was a photo of a yellow triangle inside a black box. This would be the "challenge and password" to get inside the airport. I was optimistic after reading this. We had professionals on the ground working. We were close. Then a ridiculous request came across the chat.

"We need a group photo of all 33 people combined."

"What the fuck?!" I messaged Avani. I waited to see what kind of other response that request would get on the chat. But there wasn't any. So I jumped on to give my opinion.

"Is a 33-person selfie inconspicuous enough?" Of all the Special Ops, CIA and other DoD personnel on the chat, I couldn't believe that it took a sergeant in the Army to point out how dangerous that would be. Thankfully, people agreed. Four minutes later the photo request was canceled.

A little while later, PK sent out a list of 17 names the Special Ops exfiltration team had agreed to take. The Paimans weren't on it. After all they had done to get there! They had put their faith in us. Now, they were stranded at a gas station in the middle of the night surrounded by danger on all sides.

I was fuming. In a separate chat with Avani, I raged, while she did her best to keep me calm. While I advocated to push PK to get them on the list, she kept telling me to stand down. Her time at the State Department and her exposure to the way things worked in DC helped her see there were behind-the-scenes political things going on I couldn't see.

"If we don't get in on this one, we'll try for the next one," Avani texted me.

"Fuck that, it's now or never," I replied. Politics were definitely not my strong suit.

But I knew she was right. We couldn't afford to blow our relationship with the exfiltration team or PK out of the water. If the Paimans were going to get in, we'd need them to do it.

Soon after, we got word that the Special Ops team had grabbed another family to bring into HKIA when gunfire erupted just up the road. PK told us to have the Paimans move back 300 yards. They were shutting the operation down until the threat was over.

As the sun was coming up in Kabul, the Paimans were in limbo. At about 5:45 a.m. Kabul time, PK sent a message out on the chat letting us know that a woman with CIA exfiltration experience named LT was taking over the operation. LT then sent out the list of families she was tracking for the operation. Once again, the Paimans didn't make the list.

This time I couldn't restrain myself, politics or not. I sent a direct message to LT letting her know our family was inexplicably left off her list, but had risked life and limb to go where they were told. She responded by telling me that they were only authorized to take American citizens at that point. I begged her, but she said she had her orders and couldn't violate them. I got it, but that didn't change the fact I thought it was bullshit.

Neither Avani nor I had the heart to tell "B" the news. We stalled him by saying they were waiting for the threat level to be lowered before resuming operations. Meanwhile, we were scrambling to find an alternative.

While we were doing so, we were aware the family hadn't slept in 48 hours and they were stranded and vulnerable on the side of the road. With no clear path in, we suggested that "B" tell them to get to a hotel to rest while we searched for a workaround.

"I'm sorry we couldn't get your family in today. We tried our best," I texted "B."

"It is OK sir," he texted back. His reticence told me how nervous he was.

Avani and I monitored chat rooms all that night in an effort to find a solution, but we kept coming up empty. At 10:25 a.m. EST, some 12 hours after we had sent the Paimans to a hotel, we got a new message from PK.

"Pansjhir station is back up. Get your families there now."

"Will they take us this time?" I asked.

"Get them to the station," he responded. He clearly wasn't in the mood for explanations.

Within three minutes of relaying the news to "B," the Paimans were on their way back to the gas station. Just 10 minutes later, there was a report that the Taliban were searching the station. I told "B" to stop them. "I know this is frustrating as hell," I added.

PK sent out a new challenge password. Inexplicably, it was a photo of Rosie O'Donnell. People were clearly running on fumes and punch drunk by this point. The passwords had evolved from a yellow triangle to Rosie O'Donnell. In retrospect, it was a sign that the end was near.

PK then sent another message introducing a guy named Matt as the new head of ops. I immediately messaged him and he responded, "You're in contact with the Taiwassa family right?"

"No, the Paiman family."

"Sorry brother, only AMCITS right now. I'd have them return to their safe area."

I won't bother showing my response. You can easily imagine it. I left the chat and passed the message to "B." Feeling as deflated as I ever had before, I checked in a couple of hours later and read a final message from Gabe in the NEO Comms chat.

"Stand tall friends, in one of America's darkest hours, you all provided hope to thousands and saved many of them."

That was it. Gate operations at HKIA had officially been suspended. All the gates were being forever shut and barricaded from the inside. Yes, we had provided hope to many. But, we had failed the Paimans in their moment of need.

Shift to Plan B

As devastating as this moment of realization was, we didn't wallow in it for too long. For one, we had experienced bitter disappointment during the course of Abdul and Mohammad's exfiltration, but look at how that turned out.

It also helped that "B" sent me a message that left me no choice about whether to forge on and find a solution. "There is still hope, isn't there sir?"

A lump gathered in my throat as I responded. "Yes brother there is still hope."

That hope came in the form of a conversation with Avani, who told me that Allied Airlift21 was starting to plan an overland exfiltration option out through Tajikistan. They were planning on busing people up north to Mazar-e Sharif and hiding them in safe houses until they could organize Special Forces teams to escort them across the border. I let "B" know about this option.

"It will begin in three days. I think you and your family need to have a discussion on what you think is best. It will be very dangerous as there will be Taliban checkpoints all the way to MES."

"Ugh, OK sir," he responded in an understandably disappointed and apprehensive tone. I can't imagine how afraid he must have been about the prospect of sending his mother and four siblings on a journey as perilous as the one we proposed.

During the next couple of days, Avani, Captain Minnich and I communicated frequently to discuss different options. Avani pitched an idea she had been working on with PK, our Army Ranger contact who had worked so hard to get them into HKIA.

Avani had found herself leaning on PK for emotional support. The stress of her intense work as a caseworker for Allied Airlift21 and the disappointment of not getting the Paimans out eventually led to her breaking down on the phone while she was speaking with him. After she confided in PK, he told her about another option he'd been hearing about behind the scenes.

Senator Richard Blumenthal from Connecticut had a plan in place to fly two planes into Afghanistan to pick up some high-value targets. The plane's call signs were Sayara 1 and 2. It was part of a larger plan to fly six planes into the country. Maybe she could get five seats on one of the planes.

Excited by what she heard, Avani asked for a contact number at the senator's office, which PK provided to her. She hung up thinking that of the few options available, the chance to piggyback onto a U.S. senator's operation was by far the best-sounding one out there.

Avani and Captain Minnich immediately linked up on a conference call to Senator Blumenthal's office. She fully expected a junior staffer to answer the phone, and from there she hoped to sweet talk her way to the senator's chief of staff at best.

Instead, a deep voice picked up, saying simply, "Hello." She asked if she had reached Senator Blumenthal's office.

"This is Senator Blumenthal," the voice responded. PK had given her the senator's personal phone number. Understandably surprised, Avani took a moment to compose herself, and then briefed the senator on why she was calling.

Without committing to anything, he told her he would do everything he could to help and would put her in touch with his chief of staff, Joel Kelsey. Little did she know as she excitedly hung up the phone, Avani had just put us on the path for a journey that had more twists and turns and highs and lows than many thriller novels.

As Avani was reaching out to Joel Kelsey, the curtain finally came down on the 20-year American involvement in Afghanistan. On August 30, we watched on TV as Major General Donahue took one last look around the pitch black and empty HKIA airport and stepped onto the last American military flight out of Afghanistan.

It felt like an anti-climatic moment, probably because of the work we still had ahead of us. But, to put it into perspective, 2,324 U.S. service members took their last breath on Afghan soil over that time, as did 3,917 U.S. private contractors, a fact that the Pentagon does not like to discuss, and doesn't officially acknowledge.[5]

That moment also officially confirmed that, if we were going to get the Paimans out of Afghanistan, it wouldn't be from Kabul.

The contact with Blumenthal's staff paid immediate dividends. Joel messaged Avani and told her that with the help of a woman named Alexa Greenwald from Sayara International, a U.S.–Afghan development company, his team had organized a convoy of buses leaving from Kabul to Mazar-e Sharif. They would have to pass through up to 16 Taliban checkpoints, a very dangerous route, but it was the best hope to get the family out of Afghanistan.

Joel was clearly a good guy to have on our side. As I found out later when I met him in both Ohio at my unit's HQ and in his office at the Hart Senate Office Building in D.C., he's a very affable, highly competent professional who has the one trait that many working in Washington seem to be lacking now—authentic compassion. From our first communication with him, it was clear there was nothing make-believe about his commitment to getting as many Afghan allies out as he could.

---

5   *20 Years of War*, https://watson.brown.edu, Brown University, Watson Institute for International and Public Affairs, 9/1/21.

I'm sure the fact that his boss felt just as strongly about the issue influenced him. I wouldn't become aware until later about Senator Blumenthal's own personal commitment to the cause. The senator himself was a former Marine, and he had one son who served as a Marine officer in Afghanistan and another who was a Navy SEAL. He's also a member of the Senate Armed Services Committee, which deals with issues involving our military.

Senator Blumenthal wasn't afraid to buck party lines and point out how wrong it was for our government to leave our allies behind, and he was willing to publicly call out the State Department for dragging its feet on evacuating Americans and Afghan allies during and after the HKIA mission.

He was kind enough to sit down with me in September, 2022 for this book and open up about why he became so involved in the evacuation, and later, why he co-sponsored legislation like the Afghan Adjustment Act to help pave the way for our Afghan allies to gain legal status in the United States.

Much to my surprise, he told me that his son, the Marine officer, had spent over two years trying to get the interpreter who worked with him in Helmand Province out of the country. The fact that his son had gone to law school, is a practicing attorney, has a father who's a U.S. senator, and *still* had a difficult time navigating the SIV system made him aware the system was broken before the HKIA operation even began.

"The SIV system is clearly broken," he told me. "It's not that it's intentional. But it's become so cumbersome and ineffectual. The time it takes to process an applicant is simply absurd."

His passion about fixing the broken SIV process and his belief in never leaving someone behind on the battlefield explain why he was willing to give his phone number to a complete stranger like Avani, and then gave his staff free rein to help us. What kind of senator gives out their personal cell phone number to strangers? It's safe to say not many.

With Joel Kelsey, Alexa Greenwald, Communications Director Maria McElwain, and Legislative Director Colleen Bell, firmly in our corner, we began Plan B. Despite the obvious danger of an 8–10-hour bus ride that would travel through many Taliban checkpoints, the family agreed that it was worth the risk. On the night of the 30th, we guided the Paimans to the rally point and they boarded the bus.

Before they boarded, we instructed them to delete all American-associated numbers from their cell phones and to erase any texts or communications the family had with their son "B" back in the States. They were also instructed to hide all their SIV-related documents in his mother's bra, as Muslim custom would not allow for her to be body searched. I can't imagine how embarrassing that conversation would have been for her, but I'm sure she knew it was the safest thing to do.

Finally, we asked them to check in with "B" every couple of hours to let him know they were safe, and to then immediately erase the text from their phone. With nothing else to do for the next few hours as the bus wound its way north through Afghanistan, I took the first watch to stay awake with "B," while Avani and Minnich got a little shut-eye. We were all running on fumes trying to keep up with our day jobs, while also staying laser-focused on the mission.

"B" kept me updated with reports from the bus as it journeyed north. The Taliban were boarding the buses at some stops and checking IDs and phones. We also heard unconfirmed reports out on other chats that they were scrolling through phones for +1 phone numbers and executing people on the spot if they found one. As they made their way through the checkpoints, I can speak for everyone involved when I say we were very relieved that we had stressed the need for operational security to "B's" family.

After what seemed like an eternity, we finally got word that the buses had made it to Mazar-e Sharif and the people had been dispersed to a number of different safe houses and wedding halls near the airport by a ground ops team. Having been stationed near the airport during deployment, I could almost visualize where the Paimans and others would be waiting anxiously for the next, and most important, leg of the journey.

Working with Sayara International, Senator Blumenthal's team had coordinated for two charter flights with KAM Air, the largest private Afghan airline. They were scheduled to leave at 6 p.m. on September 1.

Why would the Taliban agree to it? For the same reason people are willing to abandon their moral principles the world over: cold, hard cash.

The Taliban were technically not a declared terrorist state at that point, and the U.S. was clearly negotiating political issues with them, but negotiating with the Taliban is a political risk for any U.S official no matter how far removed they were from it. The likely scenario is that KAM Air negotiated with the Taliban, and then built that into the price they charged Sayara International for the two flights.

A Fox News reporter got wind of the operation and called Blumenthal's team for comment. A staffer told the reporter that if word got out to the Taliban, it would kick off a manhunt around the airport and innocent lives would be put in jeopardy. To their credit, they agreed not to run with the story. In this hyper-partisan, divided world we live in, that almost qualifies as a miracle.

Faced again with an immediate deadline, Avani got to work on getting the Paimans the necessary visa to clear the checkpoint at the airport and get seats on one of the planes. She made contact with a paralegal in New Jersey named Abby Carrigan, who worked as a pro bono advocate for Sheppard Mullin, an international law firm. The firm even paid the humanitarian parole fee for the family.

We knew we would have to wait for the humanitarian parole visa to process, but if we could get the family past the Taliban checkpoint at the airport, they'd be able to establish their eligibility with State Department officials in Doha, Qatar, the destination for the flights. So we did the next best thing: Avani created fake visas to fool the Taliban, and then sent them to "B" to relay to his family.

It was definitely a hair-raising solution that would have probably resulted in their deaths if they were caught. But like the Marines at Abbey Gate, how many Taliban would be able to distinguish a real document from a fake one? They were soldiers, not diplomats. Without another immediate solution, they agreed it was a risk worth taking.

In a conference call between the team that day, I reminded them of the Ben Affleck movie, *Argo,* the ripped-from-the headlines account of American officials trapped in Tehran after the Iranian revolution and seizure of the U.S. embassy. They pretended to be a Canadian film crew and created fake visas to escape from the Tehran airport under the noses of the Revolutionary Guard. If it worked then, it could work now. Plus, it gave Avani and me a good way to relieve stress: "Argo fuck yourself," we'd joke with each other to lighten the mood.

The Long Wait

As the minutes ticked down towards the scheduled takeoff, we got a message from Senator Blumenthal's office. The plane would need White House and State Department approval to land at the U.S. military base in Doha.

That wouldn't be a problem, right? After all, it was a United States senator, a sitting member of the Armed Services Committee, who helped arrange for the flight, not some shadowy CIA operative holding up a photo of Rosie O'Donnell.

The departure time came and went. So did the next day, and the next day, and the next. Our frustration and anxiety mounted as the days passed. I tried to remind myself that this was Afghanistan, and nothing ever went as planned on a Western timetable.

If we were so anxious, imagine how the Paimans and the other evacuees felt as our ground ops teams brought them food and water and shuffled them around from safe house to safe house. Every interaction was a potential deathtrap for the evacuees. Sure, the Taliban had negotiated a deal, but outside the gates of the airport, it might be a different jurisdiction with soldiers who operated by a different set of rules.

In fact, a few days into the tortuous wait, we got some intel that the Taliban had been conducting a manhunt for specific people, and had entered some of the safe houses in their search. We immediately told "B" to tell his family to not answer the door if they knocked. If they came in, present their identification, answer only questions they were asked, and have a cover story ready for why they were in Mazar-e Sharif.

Meanwhile, as they sat and waited, the Blumenthal team was exerting pressure behind the scenes to get the State Department to grant permission to land the planes in Qatar. But the reputation that

DoS had earned at HKIA for its alleged foot dragging had followed them to Mazar-e Sharif.

On September 6, Secretary of State Blinken, speaking at a press conference in Qatar about the grounded planes in MES, said, "We don't have the means to verify the accuracy of manifests, the identity of passengers onboard these planes, aviation security protocols, or where they plan to land, among other issues. And these raise real concerns."

That was enough to raise the blood temperature of Senator Blumenthal's communications director to the boiling point.

"If what we have submitted is not adequate, then the State Department's message is that they will not help Afghans to leave the country. That runs counter to the promises that Secretary Blinken and President Biden have made to our allies—to the Afghans who risked everything for our country—and we hope it isn't true," Maria McElwain said in response in a press release. "We are eager to work with the administration to ensure the safe take off of these flights," she said.[6]

Having gotten to know Maria a little since then, I can picture her sitting at her desk writing this. I wasn't there, but I know two things for sure: she had to delete a few colorful words before she hit send, and the keys on her computer keyboard were probably sore for days. She's a very nice person with a great sense of humor, but fierce in her convictions for doing the right thing.

It took some time, but holding them publicly accountable worked. Senator Blumenthal posted on Twitter that Secretary Blinken had agreed to get involved to make sure the planes got out, and soon after, we saw a *Wall Street Journal* article saying that Blinken had secured landing rights at Al Udeid Air Base in Doha for six flights, and was negotiating with the Taliban to let the flights leave.

By then, I could tell that the stress was getting to "B." On top of this, he was working two jobs, and had a wife in the late stage of her pregnancy. The on-again, off-again pattern of this mission was putting a strain on everyone's mental health, but especially his. Sitting in Toledo, Ohio, 7,000 miles away from his family, he had to try to keep them

---

6   CNN, 9/7/21.

calm as the anxiety of staying one step ahead of the Taliban built up. It needed to happen, and quickly!

On Friday, September 17, we got news that one of the two Blumenthal planes had been cleared to leave. This was a process that required—even after White House approval—coordinating with KAM Air's multiple representatives, the Al Udeid ground operations team, CENTCOM, the U.S. State Department's task force in Doha, and the Qatari Ministry of Foreign Affairs.

On multiple occasions, the Blumenthal team had secured a takeoff time with KAM Air, received clearance from the State Department's task force and CENTCOM, and negotiated landing times with Al Udeid, only for the Qatari diplomatic clearance to expire while the plane was on the runway.

This didn't just cause anxiety bordering on panic for all the people involved in the effort. On three separate occasions, the traumatized passengers on this first plane had to return to their safe houses while the team was forced back to square one, and left scrambling to secure all the necessary approvals again within the nearly impossible 36-hour time frame.

Given all the obstacles, the fact that the first plane was allowed to take off was a miracle. But it was a short-lived victory. Almost immediately after it departed and began its climb, the plane was ordered back to the airport. Apparently, its landing rights at Al Udeid had been revoked for some inexplicable reason.

It took another few days for the team to put all the ducks in a row and get another clearance for takeoff. When it finally did leave, we held our breath and tracked the plane's progress on a flight tracker, and finally exhaled and cheered in unison when it cleared Afghan airspace.

The Paimans were manifested on the next plane out. They were scheduled to leave the following evening at 6:30 p.m. But I woke up the next morning to the news that the Taliban had inexplicably scrubbed the flight. Near to breaking point by this time, the Paimans had to go back into a holding pattern. By this time, they had spent almost three weeks stuck in limbo.

Finally, two days later, there was some real movement, although it happened in the fits and starts that we had become accustomed to. The

Paimans and other evacuees were loaded onto buses this time, but, once again, the Taliban changed their mind and they were brought back to the safe houses.

Later that evening, we got a message from "B" that they had been put back on the buses and were on the move. A short while later, we received a photo of the family sitting on the bus. This was a very promising development.

Even so, I reminded myself to damper expectations and then said a prayer and asked God to let this family escape. So far, a U.S. senator's assistance hadn't been able to get them out. Maybe some divine intervention would help.

We knew there were two Taliban checkpoints on the way to the airport, and then two more inside the airport to get into the terminal. Presenting fake visas to the soldiers manning these checkpoints would be stressful enough. But then we got word that a high-ranking member of the Taliban who had been on a U.S. government "kill or capture list" was personally cross checking the manifest lists of passengers. This mission obviously had become a high priority for the Taliban.

I wasn't aware of it at the time, but among the 784 people who were on the two flights the Blumenthal team was involved with, there were former Afghan government officials, U.S. embassy employees, journalists, professors and other professionals, along with interpreters, dual-national citizens and the like.[7] The high-ranking Taliban official was more than likely looking to make sure no high-value targets slipped out under their nose.

"B" sent us a message that they passed through the first checkpoint. After that, communications from the family went silent, although we still got reports from the ground ops team. Two very anxious hours later, "B" texted us that they had made it into the terminal. They had passed all four checkpoints using the fake visas.

"Argo fuck yourself," I texted Avani.

It was a cathartic release, not a celebration, because we knew that we could only do that when the wheels touched down in Doha.

---

7   Sayara International news release, https://sayarainternational.com, 10/7/21.

At 5:20 a.m. EST we got a photo of the Paiman family sitting on the plane. The flight took off shortly after. On the flight tracker, the skies were full of dots indicating multiple airplanes in every surrounding country's airspace, but there was only one flight over Afghanistan, and the Paimans were on it.

At 7:45 a.m. I sent the following message to the team: "They officially cleared Afghan airspace." I swear I could hear their cheers from D.C. at my house in Michigan.

It was an amazing feeling. I thought back to the quote by Margaret Mead that I had put up on Abdul and Mohammad's GoFundMe page: "Never doubt that a small group of thoughtful, committed citizens can change the world. Indeed, it's the only thing that ever has."

"So fucking proud of you brother," I texted "B." He had been an absolute rock for his family for 27 nerve-wracking days. I thought back to the text he had sent me at the beginning: "Is there still hope?" I responded out loud, a lump of joy and relief now lodged in my throat. "Fuck ya brother, there's still hope."

Shortly after receiving confirmation from his family that they had made it safely to Doha, "B" sent out a group message.

"Hi all. I know this is nothing but I would like you all to know how grateful I am. It is hard to use words to convey my heartfelt appreciation to the kind help you rendered me. You all are indeed good friends, great family and awesome leaders. I am very grateful."

For 27 days of anxiety and fatigue, I was rewarded with a message that will provide me with a lifetime of peace. I'd say I was the lucky one.

CHAPTER 13

The Aftermath

After stops in Qatar, Germany, and eventually Fort Bliss in Texas to go through the entry process, the Paiman family arrived in Ohio on November 24, 2021 to live with their son and brother, Bismillah. His wife gave birth to their first child the same day. You couldn't script a better family reunion!

As just five of the 88,500 Afghans who've arrived in the United States since August 2021,[1] the story of their journey is now a part of the *#DigitalDunkirk* archive. But in my mind, it still remains almost as fresh as the days when it unfolded.

I found out later that the actress Tina Fey donated some money to fund the cost of the charter flight that got the Paiman family out of Afghanistan. Fey played a non-fictional character named Kim Barker, a *Chicago Tribune* reporter embedded in Afghanistan, in a 2016 movie called *Whisky Tango Foxtrot* (WTF for you civilian readers).

After Kabul fell, the Blumenthal team had been asked to help get one of Kim Barker's associates out of the country. Due to her involvement with the film, this request sparked a connection to Fey, which led to her making a very generous donation to help get the Mazar-e Sharif planes in the air—which I've heard cost in the neighborhood of $700,000 per flight.

But as rewarding as it is to think back on that experience, it's also sobering to remember that, while we all gave just about everything we

---

[1] Department of Homeland Security/dhs.gov/allieswelcome, Operation *Allies Welcome* website.

had to give to do right by our allies, we left many, many eligible people behind. Approximately 200,000 according to No One Left Behind. Considering how bad things are under full Taliban control now, that's a horrifying reality.

This is a fact I can't hide from. Due to my contact information getting leaked, I still get heartbreaking messages from those increasingly despondent allies trapped in Afghanistan. I still see their messages posted on social media. I still see the look in Abdul's eyes when he mentions his brother, Massoud, and his family.

Back in Afghanistan, the veneer of moderation that the Taliban presented in the first days of the takeover was stripped away as soon as international observers left. It was just as Sergeant Zielinski said about their behavior at Abbey Gate—nothing but a show.

The United Nations has documented widespread human rights abuses by the Taliban in the 20 months since their takeover. They rule with an iron fist, but their rule is not universally accepted in Afghanistan. They are contending with ISIS-K, who bitterly oppose them, but seem more content with killing Hazara and other Shi'a civilians in horrific bomb attacks, and a group called the National Resistance Front (NRF), which is led by the son of the "Lion of Panjshir," Ahmad Massoud.

The NRF operates from Commander Massoud's Panjshir Valley homeland an hour north of Kabul. Known as the cradle of armed opposition in Afghanistan, the valley is 75 miles deep, with a single road that's surrounded by 10,000-foot mountains. A trail at the far end of the valley leads up to a 14,000-foot-high mountain pass into the Hindu Kush mountains.

With this kind of topography, it's the ideal place to mount an armed opposition. Most of the 200,000 inhabitants of the small villages that dot the valley and its 21 sub-valleys are ethnic Tajik, and they're renowned as resistance fighters. The Soviets found this out when they attempted to assault the valley and root out the elder Ahmad Massoud's resistance. So too did the Taliban in the late 1990s and early 2000s.

But the conditions for armed resistance were far better then than they are now. The elder Massoud's Northern Alliance received a flow of weapons from the U.S. to combat Soviet forces, including shoulder-fired

Stinger missiles. Multiple suppliers and supply routes from neighboring countries helped equip resistance fighters opposing Taliban rule at the turn of the millennium.

Today, though, the NRF stands virtually alone. It appears that the U.S. government has decided to wipe its hands clean of Afghanistan after 20 years, 6,247 American deaths, and over $2 trillion in costs. Once that last plane flew out of Kabul, the politicians turned their attention to the newest pressing crisis.

Despite having an ally in place who could potentially reverse the devastation of the Taliban's brutal reign with no American boots on the ground and a minimal investment in arms and munitions, our government has turned its back on Afghanistan. I'd like to say I've become jaded enough to accept this rationally, but I can't.

After making contact with Vets4NRF, a U.S. veterans' organization dedicated to helping the NRF continue its fight, I received an invitation to meet with Commander Massoud at a conference in Vienna, Austria in April, 2023. If you want to meet him, book a flight and get yourself over there, I was told. It's a one-time offer.

I can honestly say I felt like I got hit with a lightning bolt when I heard the invitation. Let's face it, how many Army veterans expect to meet with the head of the opposition of a country they had deployed in a few years before? The fact that I was co-hosting *The Afghanistan Project Podcast*, which is dedicated to keeping a spotlight on the fate of our allies still left in Afghanistan, obviously had a lot to do with it.

The conference was the NRF's way of drawing attention to its continued resistance to the Taliban, which is still unrecognized as a legitimate government by almost every country on the globe. The NRF has made overtures to the Taliban to engage in discussions to create a representative government, but they've been rebuffed.

After listening to a variety of speakers for two days, I got a late-night phone call in my hotel room advising me to come down to the lobby in five minutes. After a quick walk down the street to another hotel, I was taken into a small conference room to meet Massoud.

He didn't fit the Hollywood image of a feared resistance fighter. Instead, he was friendly, open and very well-spoken. Massoud was educated in

London and attended the Royal Military Academy in Sandhurst. He looks like his father, whose face is still plastered on billboards, monuments and shop windows in Panjshir, and probably in hidden photo albums in houses all across the country.

In the half hour I spent with him, he made it clear that armed resistance is the only way to save the country from the ongoing tyranny of the Taliban. Their brutality, treatment of women and girls, and their rigid interpretation of Islam have reversed 20 years of gains, he said. They've also given haven to terrorist groups, which is precisely why the U.S. and coalition troops went there back in 2001.

The NRF claim to have the manpower to take Bagram Air Base and perhaps Kabul, but they don't have the weapons needed to hold them and eventually drive the Taliban out. Weapons and financial support; that's all they were seeking from Western allies. So far, that plea has fallen on deaf ears.

For now, though, the Taliban are firmly in control of the country, and free to do as they please. The promise of leniency for Afghans who provided assistance to American and allied troops was predictably false. They're stalking former interpreters and their families like wounded prey around the country. The Afghan allies left behind are begging for someone, anyone, to help get them out.

In late summer, 2022, the UN said it had confirmed 160 cases of extrajudicial killings by the Taliban of former government and security officials. By March, 2023, No One Left Behind said they knew of 240 confirmed cases of SIV applicants killed by the Taliban. There are surely more who've been killed we haven't heard about yet.

The sad fact is that the Taliban are dragging the country back to the Stone Age, and they don't seem to give a damn, as long as their interpretation of Islam is enforced.

They are pariahs whose government has been shunned by the rest of the world. Despite a concerted push by Taliban leaders to gain formal recognition, only Saudi Arabia, Pakistan and the United Arab Emirates have done so.[2]

In terms of providing even basic needs to the population, they don't. A United Nations report in the summer of 2022 warned that 59 percent

---

2 Brookings Institute, 9/30/22.

of the population is in need of humanitarian assistance and up to six million are in danger of starving. With a severe drought continuing for a third year, those staggering numbers continued into 2023.

The international aid that propped up the economy—40 percent of the country's GDP and 70 percent of government spending over most of the 20 years we were there[3]—has slowed to a trickle and is nowhere close to enough to meet the basic needs of the country's 40 million people. Until the Taliban meet Western demands to restore rights to females, stop punishing non-Taliban minorities and cut ties to terrorist groups, the Afghan people will be the ones who pay the price.

The decision by the Biden administration to freeze over $3 billion after the Taliban takeover has also contributed to the humanitarian crisis. A sum of money, $7 billion in total, had been deposited in the Federal Reserve Bank in New York prior to the Taliban takeover by Da Afghanistan Bank, the country's central bank. The U.S. government has authorized the release of $3.5 billion to a trust set up in Switzerland to provide humanitarian assistance to Afghans. But the remaining $3.5 billion is in legal limbo, tied up by a complex web of court cases filed by surviving family members of 9/11 victims, who in 2011 won what appeared to be a symbolic $100 billion judgment against Al-Qaeda and the Taliban for their role in planning, executing, and abetting the attacks.

Afghans in exile in the U.S. have filed their own counter lawsuits, saying that the plaintiffs in that case should not be entitled to the $3.5 billion, because it belongs to the Afghan people, not the Taliban. The Afghan people, they also correctly point out, had no involvement in the 9/11 attacks. If the U.S. wants to punish a nation-state for that, they should turn to Saudi Arabia, where 15 of the 19 attackers were from.

We know that's not going to happen. The fact is, the overwhelming humanitarian need for the money in the country outweighs any claim the 9/11 plaintiffs say they have to it, the IRAP lawsuit adds. It's hard to argue with that.

While the legal wrangling here continues, the grim reality of life under the Taliban grinds on for the most vulnerable of the Afghan population. In addition to the widespread violence, hunger, and unemployment for

---

3   United Nations Development Program report, 10/5/22.

the overall population, Afghan women and girls have lost almost all the hard-earned rights they had gained over the 20 years the Taliban were out of power.

That's left them with a sense of hopelessness. A quote I saw in a *New York Times* article sadly describes how many of them, the younger population especially, feel: "The future is dark. I feel like a bird who has wings, but cannot fly."[4]

Over 34,000 female-owned businesses have been shut down, girls' schools are shuttered, and a strict dress code requiring women to wear head-to-toe clothing in public has been enacted. The fears that Najma Sadeqi expressed in her last YouTube video before she died at Abbey Gate have come to pass. A July, 2022 United Nations report says that one to two Afghan women have committed suicide every day since the Taliban takeover.

Life is far less oppressive for the average Afghan man under Taliban rule, but their prospects for providing for their families have nosedived. The World Bank reports that the Afghan economy shrank 30–35 percent by the end of 2022 and nearly 70 percent of the population finds it difficult to pay basic household expenses.

The lucky ones, like Abdul and Mohammad's family, have family members who made it to the U.S. and other countries and have been able to secure a job and regularly send money back to help support them. Like so many immigrant stories, it's an arrangement written into their social contract.

Abdul's brother had worked in a jewelry shop, but like 700,000[5] other Afghan workers in the year after the Taliban takeover, he was laid off. The family is now completely dependent on the money Abdul is able to send. After providing them a good piece of his paycheck, he struggles to pay rent, make car payments and put food on the table for his family with his salary as a car mechanic. The people who claim Afghans are coming to this country to live on government handouts have absolutely no clue what they're talking about.

For the hunted SIV applicants left behind in Afghanistan, the ability to support themselves and their families is pretty much non-existent.

---

4   *New York Times*, 3/8/23.
5   United Nations Development Program report, www.undp.org, 10/5/22.

I can't even imagine how terrifying and depressing a life that must be; the fear of being caught by a ruthless predator mixed with the feeling of helplessness and shame that comes with an inability to provide for their families. They have only hope to cling to. Like the slim hope that a bureaucrat in America will move their SIV application up the line. Or the even slimmer hope that they receive a message to get to the airport for a flight out of Afghanistan.

If they're high-value targets for the Taliban, like one of the estimated 20,000–30,000 ANA commandos trained by U.S. Special Operations, their options are just as limited, other than the ability to put up a fight when the Taliban do find them. Or, they might choose to accept an offer from the Russian mercenary group, Wagner, which had been actively seeking out ANA commandos to fight for them in the bloodbath of Ukraine.[6]

This was one of the fears expressed in 2021 when the Afghanistan withdrawal debacle was unfolding: the soldiers we spent so much time and resources training and equipping, and then left behind, would end up fighting for terrorist groups or rogue states like Russia.

What a choice: safe passage out of Afghanistan and a paycheck that far exceeds any they could make at home, with a fair chance of dying in a country you have no quarrel with, versus a life in hiding and no prospects for the future. Option one is bad, and many Afghans still consider Russians their enemy, but who could blame anyone for choosing it over option two.

For all these allies we left behind, their problems could be solved if our politicians put aside partisan politics for a moment and did the right thing by finding a way to fast-track SIV applicants, fix the program, and bring these people to safety.

These days, I hear more and more American politicians referring to themselves and their supporters as patriots. Frankly, it makes me nauseous, because I think most of them would choose themselves and their careers over the country all day long.

But just to remind them, the definition of patriot in the *American Heritage Dictionary* is the following: "A person who loves their country and zealously supports it and its interests."

---

6   *Foreign Policy* website, https://foreignpolicy.com, 10/25/22.

Fulfilling promises to allies is in our country's interest. True patriots would do whatever it takes to get them out of harm's way. In addition to being the honorable thing to do, it supports and advances America's interests, because there will never be a time when standing alone in the world makes strategic sense.

That's why bad actors like Russia and China try so hard to split apart our alliances. That's also why you never leave your allies to wonder whether you'll have their back when they need you. Unfortunately, I think our government planted that seed of doubt in Afghanistan. But we can still try and repair the damage.

Fixing SIV and fast-tracking the process is not the impossible task that many people claim it is. I understand the immigration issue in this country is a hot-button political issue and that makes it part of a larger and much more complicated discussion. But I also recognize that some may say there are differences between an immigrant seeking a better way of life and an Afghan interpreter who risked their life in a combat environment to help American troops, and now stands a strong chance of being killed for it.

Thankfully, there are some politicians on both sides of the aisle who recognize that too. Democratic Senator Richard Blumenthal, who co-sponsored the Afghan Adjustment Act, is one, as is Democratic Senator Amy Klobuchar, the chief sponsor of the bill along with Republican Senator Lindsey Graham.

Blumenthal also sponsored the Honor Our Commitment Act 2021, which calls for the federal government to put together a cohesive strategy to streamline the SIV program, prioritize the evacuation of eligible Afghan nationals by providing remote security background checks, and identify other countries who are willing to accept them.

Unfortunately, both these bills are stalled in Congress. The Afghan Adjustment Act has broad bi-partisan support. But Iowa senator Chuck Grassley is single-handedly blocking the bill because of concerns over security screening for Afghans who came into the country after the HKIA operation.[7]

---

7 *New York Times*, September 22, 2022.

Grassley cites a December, 2021 report by the Department of Defense that said that, of the 88,500 Afghans who came into the country in the HKIA operation, nearly 50 had been flagged to have "derogatory information and cannot be located," which is defined as "potentially justifying unfavorable fitness."

Meaning there are questions about these people, but there is no evidence that they pose a terrorist threat. If you took 88,500 Americans and ran a check on them, I guarantee there would be more than 50 who had derogatory information about them. The bigger question should be why—in the age of personal information and data tracking—these people can't be located.

The SIV logjam isn't just an issue for Afghan allies still stuck over there. It's also a problem for Abdul, Mohammad, their families and the tens of thousands who are here in the United States on humanitarian parole and granted temporary protected status (TPS).

Their TPS gives them two years of eligibility to stay and work legally in the country. If they haven't found a permanent solution by that time, they can be packed up and deported. While they wait on the SIV process and a potential passage of the Afghan Adjustment Act, they're stuck in a holding pattern.

As of this writing in the fall of 2023, they still don't have case numbers, despite legal assistance from Jewish Family Services of Washtenaw County, which has been a great resource to them and other resettled families in the area. Their two-year Humanitarian Parole visas expired and they have applied for asylum to avoid deportation. The clock is ticking. It goes without saying that they're apprehensive about whether they'll be allowed to stay.

Senator Blumenthal recognizes the anxiety this creates for people who've had to leave their country and their life behind, and then acclimate to a new one—all the while not knowing whether they'll be forced to go back again.

"For Afghans on a humanitarian visa awaiting an SIV, they're in limbo. They're trying to work, send their kids to school and raise their families, yet they don't know if they'll be allowed to stay," he told me with a shake of his head. "Their fear of deportation is not illusory. It's real. People are deported every day in this country."

In a late 2022 press conference, a State Department spokesman said there were 17,000 principal SIV applications "in the pipeline." That does not include family members, which average about 4.5 per application, according to the spokesman. That totals approximately 76,500 applicants.

New Hampshire senator Jeanne Shaheen issued her own report about the program the next month and said that there were over 90,000 applicants in the pipeline. Only 272 of the applicants received approval in the first quarter of 2022, she claims.

Shaheen cited inadequate staffing at the National Visa Center in Portsmouth, N.H. as part of the reason for the massive backlog of cases. She's been critical about the SIV program's backlog since at least 2013, four years after it was created by Congress. Jeff Phaneuf, the very plugged-in director of advocacy for No One Left Behind, says the average SIV processing time is now at 628 days, despite the legislative requirement they be completed in nine months.

There are a lot of numbers to wade through to make sense of how logjammed the SIV program really is. It's hard to know which ones are the most accurate. I'd say a good rule of thumb is that the government reports low numbers and advocacy groups report high numbers.

No matter which ones you land on, it's clear there's still not a plan to expedite the process, despite the promises of the Biden administration to do that. Aside from streamlining the document process a little bit, not much has changed over the past 20 months.

That's a fact that's spelled out in federal court filings in a case known as *Afghan and Iraqi Allies Under Serious Threat Because Of Their Faithful Service To The United States v. Antony Blinken*.[8]

The case was originally brought on behalf of SIV-eligible applicants against the Trump Administration in 2018 by lawyers working for the International Refugee Assistance Program (IRAP). The suit asks the court to require the State Department to meet the nine-month adjudication period established as a requirement when the SIV program became law in 2009.

---

8   U.S. District Court for The District of Columbia, Case No. 1:18-cv-01388-TSC.

In May, 2022 case filings by IRAP and the Department of Justice (representing DoS), IRAP reports that the National Visa Center still has no plan for resolving case backlogs, and there are no clear guidelines for Afghans in the country to submit documents with consulates outside of the closed embassies in Kabul and Baghdad because they haven't formally been recognized as homeless by DoS.

Ukrainians displaced by the war in their country are entitled to work with U.S. consular services in Warsaw and Frankfurt, the suit points out, to file SIV paperwork. They were granted homeless status six days after Russia invaded their country. Yes, they deserve our support, but let's not forget who's been standing by our side for 20 years.

IRAP also pointed out in a March, 2023 press release that 117,000 Ukrainians have arrived in the U.S. through the U.S. Citizenship and Immigration Services' Uniting For Ukraine two-year temporary visa program, and the $575 fee that Afghans have to pay to apply for a similar visa was waived for Ukrainian applicants.

So it appears that our Afghan allies—who suffer the same fate under Taliban rule as Ukrainians do under Russian rule in territory they've occupied—are considered second-class immigrants. Despite economic hardship, they're made to pay the fee. Despite limited access to the internet, they're directed to submit paperwork to AfghanSIVApplication@state.gov, an email inbox that's the equivalent of a celestial black hole.

In its court filings and media releases, IRAP doesn't come out directly and accuse U.S. government officials of favoring immigrants who look like them, but they may as well have.

Citing the influx of SIV applicants from Afghanistan and Ukraine and the disruption caused by the Covid-19 pandemic, State Department lawyers have asked the Court to dismiss the IRAP lawsuit. It's still pending in federal court. Apparently, our government is throwing in the towel on fixing a broken immigration program. What a surprise.

In fact, 20 months after the HKIA operation, the issue of the fate of our Afghan allies has pretty much faded to black for our government and most politicians on both sides of the aisle. I have a theory that if they thought that the issue affected the outcome of elections, we would have seen a hard push to fix SIV. Maybe that's naivety on my part. Or is it cynicism?

Instead, it seems like the chosen option is to do little and say even less. Even about the positive aspects of the issue, like how we managed to evacuate 124,000 people in the middle of a major shit show.

I've spoken with quite a few people involved with *#DigitalDunkirk* for this book and for *The Afghanistan Project Podcast,* which I co-host with Beth Bailey, a fantastic Michigan-based news reporter and former Defense Department intelligence analyst.

Most, if not all, agree with me that our government's lack of recognition for what took place over those two or so weeks in August, 2021 is pretty unbelievable. It's almost as if they want to sweep the entire thing under the carpet, and that includes the good with the bad.

Aside from the Air Force handing out a bunch of well-deserved Distinguished Flying Crosses to the air crews who worked around the clock evacuating people, there's been very little formal recognition that it happened at all. As far as the veteran/civilian involvement, there's been hardly a peep from the State Department or Pentagon.

Which is a damn shame. Because as bad as our government's planning was, the story of *#DigitalDunkirk* is a story about what's right with this country. It demonstrated that when we put our differences aside, we can still accomplish great things. At no time was that more apparent than those weeks in August, 2021.

Formal recognition of *#DigitalDunkirk* would not only honor those achievements, it could provide a real lesson and platform for future private/public cooperation.

One of the more interesting follow-up assessments I read about the operation was by Lieutenant Colonel Laura Keenan, division chief for policy and strategy for the U.S. Army Cyber National Mission Force, which is part of Army Cyber Command.

Writing for the Modern War Institute at West Point, Lt. Colonel Keenan suggests that the lessons learned from *#DigitalDunkirk* could lead to the formation of a civilian auxiliary for the Department of Defense, much like the Coast Guard with its Coast Guard Auxiliary and the Air Force with the Civil Air Patrol.

This, she suggests, would allow the Pentagon to tap into the "unique skills, training and expertise developed in the military, while providing veterans with the camaraderie, clear purpose and mission" that service members often miss when they leave. This, she points out, "opens an aperture to the highly skilled talent that the military struggles to recruit, develop and retain."[9]

I think she's on to something. Not only would our government benefit, so would our veteran community. As she points out, it "aligns with recent trends in the veteran community to do mission-based work." That level of passion and commitment I witnessed out on the chat forums was evidence of that.

I think that sense of mission subconsciously drove me through the fatigue and frustration that came with it. Yes, I was definitely trying to help fulfill the promise we made to Abdul, Mohammad and Bismillah Paiman. That vow lay right at the surface for me.

But deeper down, I was also responding to the same higher calling that brought me into the Army at such a late age. Plain and simple, I felt the need to serve a higher purpose. Judging by the hundreds and hundreds of others who took part, I clearly wasn't alone.

Abbey Gate Reunion

The real heroes of the Kabul evacuation were the ones who stood on the front lines day after day, night after night. By now you know I'm talking about 2/1 Marines and the other service members—UK's 2nd PARA included—who bear the deepest scars.

For the survivors, life has gone on and so have they, in their own way. In the immediate aftermath of the bomb attack, they took part in a ramp ceremony for the 13 KIA American troops at the Kabul airport. Corporal Moore helped carry Navy Corpsman Soviak's casket onto the airplane for the trip home to Dover Air Force Base in Delaware.

---

9 Modern War Institute, *Digital Dunkirk: What the Afghan Evacuation Should Teach Us About the Future of Volunteer Support To the U.S. Military*, 9/22/21.

Moore is still in the Marines. He's serving as a machine-gun instructor at Pendleton now and got married in March 2022. The memories of the Kabul deployment have taken a toll on his mental health, he acknowledges. He's thought about using the mental health services offered to all of 2/1's Marines who went on the deployment, but so far he hasn't.

"My purpose of talking about this publicly is to make sure that 2/1's story gets told and that people don't forget about who died that day and what they died for," he concludes. "They gave their lives to make the lives of others better. If that's not a hero, I don't know what is."

Lance Corporal Bair remains in 2/1 Marines as well. He has received mental health services, he says, but it hasn't completely erased the guilt he feels about surviving when so many of his fellow Marines died.

Sergeant Ramirez left the Marine Corps and is now working in the HVAC industry in southern California. He still talks to "my 2/1 boys," on occasion, Zielinski especially. Life's gone on, Ramirez says, but he hasn't completely moved on from August 2021. "It didn't break me, but it cracked something inside," he says.

Sergeant Williamson left the Marines and is now at the Houston Police Department Training Academy. Despite leaving the Corps and moving halfway across the country, he's still having trouble sleeping. He too, has survivor's guilt. "I feel like I could have done more to save people," he says.

He also has a message for anyone who thinks that war is as bloodless as it's often depicted. "Today's society thinks war is a video game. That it's cool. But it's not. People die. Shit's real."

Air Force Major Lefaivre and his wife were on the verge of bringing their third child into the world when we spoke in early November 2022. He recognizes his great blessings, but still can't help thinking about the kids he saw at HKIA.

The baby that Sergeant Gee was holding in the viral photo a couple days before she was killed at Abbey Gate: he was the one who handed it to her. The parents were never identified, and when he went to the HKIA hospital later to check, he was told the baby had been evacuated to Norway.

Sometimes he thinks of HM3 Soviak, the Navy corpsman who was giving aid to an Afghan woman and her child when the bomb went off, killing all of them. "We called him the Pied Piper because he always had a trail of kids following him everywhere. He was just a super nice guy, and those kids sensed that."

Sergeant Zielinski is still in the Marines. He rotated out of Weapons Company and now works for Marine Logistics Group at Camp Pendleton, where he helps conduct combat skills training with engineers, EOD and other non-infantry units.

The new assignment and passage of time since HKIA hasn't dimmed his appreciation for the brothers he served with during the deployment. "I was so fucking proud to be a part of that platoon," he says.

He has two children now and is clearly a family man. That's definitely helped dull the memories, but despite seeking out mental health services, he has trouble sleeping. That little girl's green eyes still haunt him.

When I got ahold of him and told him about Abdul and Mohammad, his reaction was something I'll never forget. He can explain way better than I can.

"When I heard about Abdul and Mohammad and how they're in the States with their families and they're doing well, I lost it. It gave me a chance to release all the anger and grief I've been holding in. To know that what we did mattered, that all that shit that happened wasn't in vain. Honestly, it means the world to me."

So when I asked him if he'd like to come to Michigan and meet everyone, he didn't hesitate. He was planning to go home to Illinois on leave in early October. His family's home was about a five-hour drive from Ypsilanti. And just like that, after a few phone calls and emails, Abdul, Mohammad and I would get to meet the man who was responsible for getting them out of Afghanistan.

He came with his father, a guy who couldn't be any prouder of the son he raised. I gave him a big hug, as if we had been brothers our whole lives. Abdul and Mohammad cooked up a big feast of delicious Afghan food. The kids were all there, smiling shyly at the new American guys and running around like the care-free kids they've grown into.

It was a great get-together. Abdul and Mohammad couldn't stop thanking him for what he had done for them. Sergeant Zielinski was visibly moved and grateful for the invitation and the chance to see with his own eyes that something good had come out of his time at Abbey Gate. It wouldn't bring the 13 American KIA back or any of the others who died there, but it was something good, and that's something to hang on to.

Mohammad's oldest son, Elias, 8, said he recognized him from Abbey Gate. It must have been pretty surreal for him to see the same sweat-soaked, dirt-crusted, heavily-armed Marine who got his family through the chaotic nightmare at HKIA sitting in Michigan at his dining room table in civilian clothes breaking bread with his family.

For me, it was the final chapter in a true-life epic story that I'll carry with me forever. There's no way I can forget the friends I made and the experiences we shared. After coming home from deployment, #DigitalDunkirk allowed me to stay in the fight for a better Afghanistan, and they were the soldiers next to me in battle. No matter where we go and how long it's been since we've been in contact, we'll always have that bond.

Earlier in the year, Senator Blumenthal's team—Joel Kelsey, Maria McElwain and Colleen Bell—came to Ohio with Avani Singh to accept an award from my unit for their heroic assistance in getting the Paiman family out of Afghanistan. Like the reunion in Michigan, it was fantastic to see everyone meet and connect. The unity created during that harrowing month will never be broken.

The story's not over though. The fight still goes on to get all of our Afghan allies out. The people at No One Left Behind keep pushing the boulder uphill in their effort to get our government to uphold the promise we made to our allies.

A number of the nonprofit groups that formed independently have now banded together into larger groups to pool resources and their collective knowledge and mission tactics. Allied Airlift21, Task Force Pineapple, Team America and dozens of others have formed the Afghan Evac Coalition, www.afghanevac.org, while a group of 16 Special Operations Forces-focused groups and others like Save Our Allies have formed the Moral Compass Federation, www.moralcompassfederation.org.

Hopefully these groups and engaged politicians like Senator Blumenthal will be able to exert more pressure on Congress and the White House to finish the job we started and bring all of our Afghan allies home. It is, after all, our American promise.